A Gathering of Cats

by Era Zistel

J. N. TOWNSEND PUBLISHING
EXETER, NEW HAMPSHIRE

◆◆◆

Cover design by Martha E. Raines.

Printed in the United States by Bookcrafters.

Published by
J. N. TOWNSEND PUBLISHING
12 Greenleaf Drive
Exeter, New Hampshire 03833
(603) 778-9883

Original paperback edition.
First Printing.

Some of the essays in this book were published in slightly different forms by the following magazines: *New York Sunday News, Reader's Digest, World Youth, Down East, Cat Fancy.*

◆◆◆

Library of Congress Cataloging-in-Publication Data
Zistel, Era.
    A gathering of cats / Era Zistel.
        p. cm.
    1. Cats—Anecdotes. 2. Zistel, Era. I. Title.
SF445.5.Z57 1993   93-13155
636.8–dc20   CIP

ISBN 1-880158-00-0 $11.95

Contents

Foreword by an Ailurophile 1

The Reprieve 11

Cat Friends 21

The Revenant 29

The Cat That Could 39

The Little Ghost 47

The Saga of Squeak 53

The Boob 59

A Gathering of Cats 67

Moire 75

The Mother Cat 81

The Wild Cat 89

There Was a Cat 101

A Cat by Another Name 107

The Problem Cat 113

other books by
Era Zistel

Gentle People

Wintertime Cat

Orphan

A Cat Called Christopher

Treasury of Cat Stories

Golden Book of Cat Stories

Golden Book of Dog Stories

The Good Year

Hi Fella

The Dangerous Year

Thistle

Good Companions

Thistle & Co.

♦♦♦   ♦♦♦   ♦♦♦

A Gathering of Cats

Foreword by an Ailurophile

My attitude toward cats is much like that one has toward relatives. You not only recognize but complain about their faults. Yet let anyone call attention to those faults or even so much as agree with you while you are complaining about them, and you are fighting mad. That's how it is with me and cats.

Perhaps the reason for my always coming to their defense is that so many of them are poor relations, unwanted, scorned, neglected. If what is considered a more useful creature, say a horse, is mistreated, the perpetrator of the deed is either arrested or given a trouncing by someone bigger or stronger. The cat is seldom defended by anything but a sharp tongue.

In a book I once had the misfortune to read I came across this passage:

"The track of the house cat is too well known to need description. If it is found anywhere in hunting grounds, parks, etc., the finder will confer a benefit on lovers of nature and its feathered denizens if he, where possible, will set a trap baited with fish or cheese; or if there is a chance fill the 'varmint's' anatomy with pellets from a shotgun or a .22 rifle, or cut it in two with a big rifle bullet, he should never fail to do so. It may seem like a waste of powder and lead, but it is not, for in my opinion there is no more harmful creature afoot or awing than the domestic housecat outdoors."

I read in this same book:

"All lovers of our feathered song-birds kill the weasel at every opportunity, believing it to be one of the deadliest enemies of bird life. Considering, however, the number of injurious rodents it kills, it is doubtful if this 'little martin' is, on the whole, more destructive than useful."

I find myself wishing I could ask this man, who, I am vindictive enough to hope, has gone by now to a happy hunting ground where there is an overabundance of cats and not a single trap or gun or any other weapon at his disposal, "Are you not guilty of discrimination? Does the cat play no part in maintaining the balance in nature? Is he to be given no credit for weeding out weaklings, or praise for the number of 'injurious rodents' he dispatches?"

It is true that a "house" cat that is well fed but allowed to roam day and night, possibly soon to meet up with disaster, may do some indiscriminate killing. But the cat entirely on his own kills simply because he is hungry, the exception being that a female may do so by instinct in order to feed and train her young, even if she has no young. In contrast, the species we call human kills purely for fun, because it is a "sport" he finds enjoyable.

Yes, the well fed "house" cat may torture his prey. But the human? Here's another excerpt from the sportsman's book:

"The animal can be confined to its hole by tying a piece of paper or rag to a stick and placing it not less than two feet from the entrance, which will prevent its leaving the hole for several days, and by this ruse I have actually starved two of them to death. Each one died about eight feet from the scarecrow—about five feet inside the hole, which was examined daily—one during the nineteenth, the other during the twenty-second day of their imprisonment."

Not by any stretch of the imagination could a cat be accused of inflicting such exquisitely refined and prolonged torture as this. To my mind, the world would benefit if such "sportsmen" were similarly trapped and starved. Unfortunately, they are actually given license to roam the woods in the fall of the year.

In contrast to the dismissal of the cat as just a destructive varmint, there's the more common view giving him unusual attributes. He is, it is said, "mysterious." We find that word used in book titles, stories, articles, anything pertaining to the cat.

Is he really mysterious? After close association with felines over many years, I think I've come to know them pretty well—my own, that is. To make such a broad statement about the species as a whole would be presumptuous. Let's say I know my own cats as well as I know my human friends. In all relationships there is some element of the unknown.

Sometimes I don't know what my friend is thinking.

Similarly there are times when I look into a cat's eyes and haven't the slightest idea of what his thoughts might be. I know when he is pleased, happy, excited, out of sorts, unhappy, angry, or simply bored. But there are times when I cannot fathom the reason for his behavior. Why, for instance, does he, even though I am fairly sure he loves me, suddenly, while purring madly, make an unprovoked attack on my ankle?

In all good conscience we must admit that the cat is no more mysterious than any other animal, including man. However, there is something mysterious *about* him, surrounding him like an aura. It is our attitude toward him.

Those of us who love him give various reasons for our predilection. He is so beautiful. So are other animals. He is so graceful. In this respect, too, he is not unique. He is—what? We cannot give any truly adequate reason for our love. It simply exists, an unfathomable mystery.

Similarly, the loathing of cats cannot be explained. Other animals may be repellant to humans because they are ugly, vicious, have bad reputations, any number of comprehensible reasons. But no other animal than the cat will cause a man to pale, swoon, lose consciousness, fall down in convulsions, simply because a cat is somewhere in the vicinity. This is a mystery indeed, but so far from rare that it has been given a name, "ailurophobia." The opposite, the overweening love, also has a name, "ailurophilia." Both are inexplicable, the two halves of a mystery that is in us, not in the cat. Sometimes I suspect he may be just as baffled by it as we are.

More than once, in dark hours, I have thought that those of us who love animals are cursed, destined as we are to be hurt again and again, until our hearts are so covered with scars the wonder is that they can still beat. But we are also blessed with warm, comforting, undemanding friendships, of a special poignancy because we know they will be brief.

I'd much rather be an aelurophile than suffer the discomforts of the aelurophobe. And I'd rather be subject to the hurts of love than the drabness of indifference. The aelurophobics have my understanding and sympathy—they can't help being as they are. The emotionally deprived have my pity.

When we lived in New York the cats used to sing in the courtyard down below, a recital that frequently was interrupted and had to change location when bottles, tin cans and light bulbs were thrown down. The wrath of the other human residents in the apartment house was something I could not understand, for the sounds the cats produced were to me not so unpleasant as their own cacophony that sometimes blared far into the night. In fact, I often wondered what animals whose ears are assaulted must think of our yelling, moaning, groaning, caterwauling, shrieking that, inexplicably, we call music, or the incredible racket we make at baseball games and other sporting events, as well as—since we seem to be going deaf—the shouting we resort to in ordinary conversation.

The cats who favored us with their concerts lived in a building that had been left vacant, probably in anticipation of its being torn down to make way for a highrise, about two doors from ours. What went on inside that building could only be guessed at, but sometimes we saw kittens scamper through a broken window, or taking sustenance from mamma sunning herself on a ledge. How large the family was I could only determine by making a swift count, up to twenty-five, when a waiter in a restaurant on the next street leaned over the back fence and called, "Here, kitty, kitty!"

At once there was a great rush, cats of all sizes and colors plus one rat, and the waiter would dump over the fence a great mound of the restaurant's leftovers. I often wondered, later, what eventually became of that commune, of the benefactor who fed it, of the building that housed it.

Of course we soon acquired two cats of our own, Speck and Toffie, progeny of the big black cat in the fruit store, a proud fierce mother she was. Neither kitten resembled her. Speck was an outrageous showoff, fully aware of how alluring she was with her gleaming black coat, dainty while slippers and immaculate shirt front. Whenever she could attract an admiring eye she posed prettily, and her favorite pasttime was to sit on the window ledge to display herself to the cats in the courtyard below, gloating over the lust she saw in their eyes.

Her next most favorite occupation was jumping. Always after she had been missing for a while we worried that she might have taken the hazardous leap into the courtyard, but finally, after anxious calling, we would hear a rustling on top of the bookshelves or the mantelpiece on the kitchen cupboard and a saucy head would peer down, daring us to come and get her. For peace of mind, then, and hoping to be warned in time to save a vase from crashing off the mantel, she was given a collar with a little bell, which she wore with pride because it attracted still more attention.

Her brother Toffie, more white than black, was dissimilar to her in every way, a solemn gentleman almost ludicrously affectionate, foregoing even a tempting morsel of food to swoon under a caressing hand.

Our third acquisition, Scorpio, was not attractive, a poorly marked tortoiseshell, her face splotched by a carelessly applied paintbrush, a shy, lonely creature neglected by an indifferent owner. That was why we took her in. Thus I can understand humans who reject adoptable children in an orphanage to select one clearly labeled "there's no use." And, in time, we came to believe her beautiful. So I can understand, too, those doting parents who display with pride their ill-favored offspring, while viewers surreptitiously shake their heads.

Scorpio wasn't even lovable. Having survived by sheer luck in a hostile environment, she was moody, given to withdrawn brooding, sliding from under our caresses to hide in corners or under chairs to gaze at us with wide-eyed mistrust. But with the arrival of her kittens, conceived in some unfortunate encounter when she was still too young, she came to know our intentions were friendly and she gave us her trust. Then when Toffie showed no antipathy toward her squirming offspring but rather enjoyed lying with them, guarding them while she ate and groomed herself and took a stroll, she actually began to find life somewhat pleasurable.

Of course we kept her kittens. Demi inherited her passion for cleanliness, and some peculiarities. Never did

I have to look out the window to find out whether it was raining. He always knew, and told me so with loud complaints, even though he suffered no discomfort. He also grumbled when the apartment was, in his opinion, too warm or too cold, when his favorite pillow was misplaced, whenever anything needed righting, most vociferously if I delayed in doing the righting. It was his firm belief that I had the power to turn off the rain, brush away the clouds, make the sun come back to shine on the window ledge, modify the temperature, perform other miracles as required. I found my failure to live up to his high esteem somewhat embarrassing.

His brother was named Elly because we knew a little boy who couldn't say "yellow." Although he and Demi were similar in color they were unlike in every other way. Demi was dainty and meticulous in his grooming. Elly was huge, clumsy, and always just a trifle dusty. Whenever he could catch me sitting down, not often enough to please him, he overflowed on my lap.

There came a time when our landlord, who had been tolerant of our feline surplus because he owned four dogs, began to show signs of disapproval after he'd reduced his holdings, and we feared that in order to remain in his good graces we'd have to cut down on ours. Elly was the one chosen to go.

The owner of the grocery store on the corner had been asking us for a cat to reduce his mouse population. Elly had never seen a mouse and was so lazy that he'd probably have said "pleased to meet you," then gone back to snoozing. But his size was impressive. The grocer promised to treat him well, even allow him to decorate the store window. So Elly was coaxed into a stout cardboard box, and I shed guilty tears over his departure.

Almost immediately the grocer returned. He hadn't gone even halfway to the corner when the cardboard box had exploded, Elly had emerged with a mighty hiss and streaked off in the direction of home. The next morning we spied him in all his golden glory sitting in the courtyard, an assortment of legitimate inhabitants gathered around to view him with admiration and respect.

In good conscience we could not claim to have rescued him, for he showed no evidence of needing our assistance, but thinking we had done so made us feel better. So did our firm "no" to the grocer when he asked for another cat.

Then, braving the landlord's wrath and the possibility of becoming homeless, we acquired Salambo, when I made the mistake of visiting a crowded, noisy, not too clean animal shelter. There she was huddled in a corner, a little heap of misery, her long white coat dirty and matted, her belly swollen in the last stages of pregnancy. How could I look into those doomed eyes and just turn away? The manager of the shelter hastened to provide a box.

Demi, Elly and Toffie and Speck found the disreputable addition to our family most distasteful, but assumed an air of indifference. Alas, Scorpio and Salambo were instant enemies, although Salambo could not have wished it so. All she wanted was peace and quiet. Perhaps Scorpio was jealous because it was most evident that Salambo was a lady fallen from high estate. Or she may have resented all the attention the poor creature received, to comb and brush her tangled fur.

However, the birth of Salambo's kittens brought an abrupt change, triggering a rebirth of Scorpio's instinct for motherhood. There followed a distressing interval of baby stealing. The little things were carried squalling from here to there and back, hidden in corners, repossessed, stolen from Salambo's box again and again, until at last an accord was reached. Mother and foster mother declared a truce, settled down together in one box with kittens in a happy mound between them.

Those were the cats we had in that city apartment, one of the reasons why we moved to the country. In the country there were more, many more. Here are some of their stories, as told when they occurred.

Salambo

The Reprieve

His name was Christopher Hudson. He was my very first cat. He cost twenty-five cents.

It was one of those strange coincidences that makes one wonder whether we might not be pieces in a chess game, one of many being maneuvered, perhaps for the enjoyment of a master hand.

I was then living in Manhattan, just outside Greenwich Village. I was lonely, not for people—there were too many of them—but for a part of me that was missing. I had seen a cat in the window of a small neighborhood grocery store languishing in the afternoon sunlight, stretched out in serenity, sure of its place in the world and the goodness of life. I had passed by often and stopped to gaze into the half-closed, friendly amber eyes, and felt something between us that I needed to make me complete.

What I needed was a cat.

In the Village, somewhere west of Sixth Avenue—those in residence did not refer to it as Avenue of the Americas—there was, I was told, a shop that sold cats, regular cats, not the very decorative but unidentifiable

Christopher Hudson

bundles of fur so favored by many people. What my hands wanted to feel was not the softness of fluff, but the firmness of bone and the warmth of living flesh. What my eyes wanted to see was the ripple of muscles in graceful movement, the exquisite curving of their lines in repose.

So one day I turned off Sixth Avenue and walked west to locate the pet shop in the Village. The hand maneuvering the pieces on the chess board placed me on a street corner just as three boys were approaching it. Seeing me, one of the boys shouted, "Hey, lady, you want to buy a kitten?"

The little thing clutched to his breast was grey and white, its grey jacket buttoned over a white shirt front, its stubby plump tail made definitive with a tip of white. It stared at me with baby blue eyes full of infant resignation and opened its mouth in a soundless mew of appeal.

The boys were more than satisfied with the quarter I dug out of my purse, and went whooping off. The little bit of flesh and bone covered with smooth baby fur burrowed into my armpit, heaved a great sigh and started to purr. We were standing on the intersection of Christopher Street and Hudson Street.

That's why he was named Christopher Hudson.

Special though he was to me, he was in fact just an ordinary kitten, comforting when he sat on my chest, paws primly tucked under him, fathomless eyes looking uncritically into mine, a mercifully silent consolation in times of hurt or grief, an entrancing performer with tossed paper balls or snaked pieces of string, a sometimes annoyance when his youthful expenditure of energy sent objects flying off tables, when in mischievousness pens and pencils filched from the strictly forbidden desk top were hidden in such inaccessible places as the farthest corner under the bed.

He was clever, soon learning that he could wheedle me into good humor with a soulful stare or a beguiling antic, flung over on his back, legs all at odds with each other, tender white belly offered for caressing, head tilted at a rakish angle certain to provoke a chuckle.

He was smart enough to learn a number of words. Those that earned immediate response were, of course, "Are you hungry?" but "Go to bed" was also favored, because this told him that soon I would be sleeping, and he could settle down where he most liked to be, in the crook of my bent knee. The single word he respected and knew he should obey instantly was "No." This meant he was doing something wrong, sometimes when he didn't know what.

He grew into a cat, acquiring nobility of stance, a confident, grave dignity, and became a good companion, a friend, a confidant, willing always to listen, never bored, never complaining about repetitions, never contradicting and, of course, never violating a confidence or divulging a secret.

When I returned home he was always there on the other side of the door, waiting to greet me. I came to expect that, take it for granted, so when he was not there one afternoon I was at first puzzled, then a little hurt, then concerned. What was wrong?

Nothing, apparently. As soon as I spoke his name he came to arch his body against my legs, but in that action of devotion there was a certain remoteness, a lack of enthusiasm. He's taking me for granted, too, I thought. He's just as sure I will come home as I am that he'll be here. That's natural enough, I suppose—an eventuality to be expected.

While I read he sat on my chest as usual, his paws neatly tucked in, his purr vibrating against my heartbeat. And that night, after the routine kneading of the blanket and the obligatory turning around three times, he settled in the crook of my knee. The next morning he responded as usual to "Are you hungry?" but did not eat with his typical zest and left some of the food on the plate. Well, we all experience an occasional falling off of appetite. It was nothing to worry about.

That afternoon I told myself not to expect him to be waiting on the other side of the door, and he was not. Nor did he come to me when I called.

"You're a fine one," I said when I found him lying on the bed. He answered by opening his mouth, but no sound came out, and I had a stab of misgiving. Then he got up and stretched and yawned. "You're just lazy," I said with relief, and he blinked as if in agreement.

The next afternoon he was not at the door, nor was he on the bed. I had to hunt for him, and finally found him on the floor, under the sofa. I tried to lift him out, and with a little cry of protest he bit my hand, not hard, just enough to hurt my feelings. When I put him on the bed he struggled out of my grasp, went to the edge, jumped down, and fell on his side. Almost immediately he was up again, but he had trouble walking. His back legs seemed sluggish, unwilling to respond when he tried to move them.

The veterinarian couldn't take us until the next day. By then Christopher Hudson was helpless. The back legs would not even bend. He gazed at me with misery in his eyes.

"Please eat," I begged, holding the dish with one hand and his head with the other. He did eat, and drank some water. That was a good sign, I thought. But when we got to the hospital the vet tried to bend the legs, ran probing fingers down the spine and shook his head.

"Paralysis, possibly progressive. Maybe not progressive, but not reversible. He won't walk again. I'm sure you don't want him to have that kind of a life."

"If he must die," I said, "I want it to be without fear, in the peace and quiet of his own home. I want to take care of it myself."

The veterinarian, a kindly, understanding fellow, nodded, took an envelope from his desk, a bottle from a shelf, and dropped two pills into the envelope.

"One should be enough," he said. "But just in case …"

Animals are said to have a strong homing instinct. Christopher Hudson knew we were going back. Half a block away he started crying, and at our door ended up with what sounded like a shout of triumph.

He fought to get out of the carrier, dug his claws into the carpet to drag himself across the floor, heading for the bed. I put him on it and he washed himself with impatient licks here and there, trying, I suppose, to rid his fur of the vet's obnoxious medicinal smell. Then he sighed deeply, closed his eyes and slept.

This would be a good time, I thought. He'd hardly

know. I took the envelope from my purse, shook out the two pills, held them in my hand, then put them back. Tomorrow, I thought. Tomorrow. Let us have one more day.

He ate his breakfast while I held the dish with one hand, his head with the other, and afterward, lying flat, washed his face. I put clean bedding under the stiff body, bathed those parts of him he could not reach, and took the two pills out of the envelope.

Then I couldn't.

"Forgive me, Chris," I begged. "I am a coward. I just can't. Give me one more day."

This was at a time when I was having trouble with my back, the result of an old injury, and miraculously I'd found a chiropractor willing to make house calls. He was a nice fellow, gentle, soft-spoken, a native of Columbia just establishing himself in New York. He gave me the usual treatment, packed up his equipment, went to the door, stopped, and returned to stare at Christopher Hudson lying in his box near the bed.

"There is something wrong?"

I told him about the paralysis and my lack of courage in facing the inevitable.

"Please, no," he said. "Wait a little. Let me see what I can do. I will not charge."

He knelt beside Christopher Hudson, who looked at him as if they were old friends, responding perhaps to the caressing voice, perhaps to the sympathy that he sensed.

"We will see, brave little man. We will try to make you well."

He came three times a week. Christopher Hudson

greeted him with little cries of welcome, and purred as the hands ran over his body.

I threw away the pills.

Actually there was no reason for optimism. Christopher Hudson was still paralyzed, helpless. But he looked at the man with such faith in his eyes that a matching faith grew in me. Then one day he hissed and growled, embedded his claws in the kindly hand and bit. I was horrified, but the man chuckled and nodded.

"Good! Good! You are beginning to feel a little, eh? See, there is slight, very slight movement. Yes, little man, I know it is painful, this return, but you will walk again, you will walk."

And he did.

Day after day Christopher Hudson purred, then hissed, growled, scratched and bit. Day after day the man said, "No matter, no matter," washed the blood from his hand, allowed me to treat the wounds with disinfectant.

Christopher Hudson drew the stiff legs up, kicked, pushed against them, managed to raise his body, stood, took a few clumsy steps, fell, stood again. Then came the day when, with a happy cry, he greeted the man at the door.

"That is my payment," the man said, once again refusing an offer from me. "And now, my little man, we must say goodbye. It has been a pleasure to know you. Walk. Get strong. Be happy."

Shortly after that we moved, out of the city, into a little house in the country, surrounded by woods. Christopher Hudson was ecstatic. Each day we took a walk, sometimes even in the rain. At first he was slow and clumsy going over the rough ground, but gradually, more rapidly than I'd dared hope, he became agile. The first time he climbed a little way up a tree I laughed with delight, and, descending, he responded with a kitten-like caper that was almost graceful.

As he came to know the woods his confidence increased, and when I was busy he started going off on his own. He would be gone for perhaps an hour, or two, and when he returned would have much to tell me, in long, excited sentences that ended only when he ran out of breath. I would listen gravely, or with awe if the gleam in his eyes told me he had had an unusual experience, or sometimes with amusement if the narrative seemed to warrant such a response. Often I wished I could know what the stories were that he told with such earnestness, what strange encounters, what fascinating adventures he had had.

Then one day, late in the fall, there must have been a bad one, because he did not return.

I called and searched, in widening circles, until the area I covered became too large and the waiting had stretched into weeks. That's how it is in the forest. It guards its secrets well. I was never allowed to know what that last adventure of his had been.

I sat on a rock where often we had sat side by side to contemplate the mysteries of the universe, trying to find a way to accept a loss that I knew would have been inevitable anyway, sooner or later.

Memories crowded in.

Christopher Hudson as a merry little kitten, impish, laugh-provoking, bounding after paper balls, chasing snakes of string. Christopher Hudson, dignified, solemn, sensing my every mood, listening attentively to my every word. Christopher Hudson not waiting for the door to open fully, thrusting a paw out through the crack to greet me. Christopher Hudson lying on my chest purring. Christopher Hudson lying helpless, gazing up at the hand that held the death-dealing pills.

Then I knew how it should be.

He had been given a reprieve, had enjoyed a whole summer of happiness, of unlimited freedom, of glorious adventure.

Those were the memories to hold on to.

Cat Friends

The cat is a loner. He is aloof, indifferent, interested only in creature comforts, good food, a warm place to sleep. He is also mysterious, whatever that may mean.

How this conception of the cat came into being, and why it is perpetuated (probably by self-appointed authorities who actually have no real acquaintanceship with cats) is a mystery in itself. Nothing could be further from the truth.

Take Meenie, for instance.

Rescued by good Samaritans from almost certain death in a busy city street, he had already lost one eye, either by accident or a deliberate act of cruelty (as suggested by his terror whenever a match was struck). Having become a hardened street fighter, accustomed to warding off attacks, he misunderstood my proffered friendship and reacted so violently that a blanket had to be thrown over him to protect me. That's why he was named Meanie, which, after evidence of good behavior, was modified by a slight change in spelling and an addition of the prefix, Eenie.

Tough though he was, there were times when he showed signs of having once known and responded to kindness. Whenever a man with a certain resonance in his voice paid a visit, Eenie Meenie would run to greet him joyfully, then turn away in disappointment. Sometime in his past life, perhaps all the way back in dimly remembered kittenhood, he had loved someone with such a voice.

In time, after my good will had earned his trust, the love was bestowed on me with such fervor that pleasing me became his major concern. Never was my authority disputed. My command "No" was always instantly obeyed, no matter what activity it stopped.

Toward the other cats in the family he was mostly indifferent, as indeed, they were to him, with the exception of a frail little fellow about half his size who answered to the unlikely name of Iffy.

Iffy, too, had had a close brush with death, having been rescued, just barely, from a fire. When brought to us he seemed to be suffering from such a bad cold that on the spur of the moment he was given the name Sniffles, which he disdained to acknowledge with even the twitch of an ear. To win his approval this name was shortened to Sniff, but only when reduced to an absolute minimum of two letters did it meet with acceptance. But If? Who ever heard of a cat, or anyone, called If? To avoid misunderstanding and tiresome questions, then, a minor alteration was made and he agreed to answer to Iffy, even with a certain amount of enthusiasm at dinnertime.

Possibly made paranoid by his terrifying experience in the fire, Iffy was so timid that any unexpected movement or sudden noise would send him off in panic to hide wherever he could. So alliance with the tough street fighter seemed most unlikely, yet he took one look at Eenie Meenie and Meenie took one look at him, and it was as if they had known each other all their lives. At once they were fast friends.

Like overgrown kittens they thudded through the house playing tag, or rolled over and over in wrestling matches until finally by mutual consent they stopped in the middle of a game, made a trip to the kitchen for a snack, then leapt up on the chair they had claimed as their property to share a nap.

Alas, their companionship, so nearly perfect, was short-lived. The fire that had damaged Iffy's psyche had also damaged his body. What had seemed like only a bad cold developed into severe lung damage, and at last he quietly withdrew from life.

Unlike many other species, who give aid to the dying members of their kind by hastening departure with cruel assaults, the cat, perhaps as a result of close association with man, tends to show respect toward the terminally ill. With deferential gravity other members of the family made detours around the box in which Iffy lay dying. Meenie passed by often and stopped to peer in. Ordinarily he would have hopped in to share a friendly nap. But now, perhaps sensing the presence of death and Iffy's need to be alone, he only hovered nearby.

When at last the box was closed and carried away, he made no attempt to follow. Nor did he cry. Not once had

I ever heard him cry. He was a stoic who accepted whatever the situation offered, even sat patiently beside an empty food dish waiting for someone to notice he was hungry. Only in one way did he protest against Iffy's departure. Meticulously clean as a rule, he sat down in the middle of the floor and made a puddle.

A few days later optimism set in, and he prowled around the house almost constantly, peering under chairs and tables, looking behind doors, crooning invitingly for Iffy to come join him. Many days passed before he gave up the search and resigned himself to loneliness as he often had to hunger. Hunched on the chair he and Iffy had shared, he sat for hours staring at nothing.

Among our other cats there was a big cream-colored fellow named Kermit, a stray who had joined the family the previous winter. Having noticed cat tracks in the snow, I'd kept watch and finally caught sight of him picking up crumbs fallen from the bird feeder, had set a Have-a-heart trap and brought him into the house. Almost immediately he had won over the other members of the family with his imperturbable good nature. He gave love to everybody— until the arrival of Coco. Then for him everybody else ceased to exist.

Coco's arrival was so similar to Kermit's that it was like the rerun of a movie. I noticed tracks in the snow, set the trap, and in no time brought him into the house.

A big cream-colored male so like Kermit as to be his double, he was, like Kermit, so affable that other members displayed no objection to his joining the family. Kermit

Kermit and Coco

stared at him. He stared at Kermit. Then, just as it had been between Meenie and Iffy, there was instant bonding.

Their devotion to each other was downright unbelievable. Never did one go anywhere without the other. Side by side they walked, so close together that they might have been a double image of just a single cat. At the window they sat together posed identically, their heads always turning in unison to follow movements in the world outside. Each evening, as soon as they had had their dinner, they climbed up on the chair that was theirs and tended to their grooming, considerately washing each other in such hard to get at places as under the chin and on top of the head. Then, lying close together, they spoke softly to each other and purred, until at last, in sound sleep, Kermit proved that they were not identical. He snored.

Lurking on the outskirts of this enviable relationship, Meenie would work up enough courage, every once in a while, to join the two of them on the chair. They were never hostile, only indifferent. For a few moments they would tolerate his presence. Then with one accord they would jump down from the chair and go to the kitchen, ostensibly for a bite to eat. Meenie would follow meekly, and while he was busy munching cat chow or drinking milk they would slip back to resume their exclusive communion on the chair.

Alas, such accord was probably too perfect to permit continuation. Kermit sickened and had to be hospitalized. Coco, suddenly bereft, almost went mad. Day and night he paced incessantly from room to room, in and out, back and forth, calling, begging, howling for Kermit to return, lashing out in fury if one of the other cats got in his way because it was not Kermit. Then on the sixth night of his anguish there was a telephone call from the hospital. Kermit had died.

For a while Coco was the same as before. Then he became unaccountably quiet. Lying on the chair where at this hour he and Kermit always had been together, he seemed to sleep, and in his sleep, as if in a dream, he purred and talked in barely audible cries of pleasure. So it was on all subsequent evenings.

Meenie noticed the change. After observing closely for several evenings, he took courage enough to join Coco, but squatted on the very edge of the chair, so as not to be objectionable. Then when Coco seemed to be sound asleep he crept closer, until he could bury his nose in Coco's fur.

Little by little the following nights he grew bolder. As soon as Coco jumped up on the chair he jumped, too, but took care to remain a respectful distance, crouching to make himself as small as possible. Slowly, slowly, the distance diminshed and his body relaxed, until finally he lay at ease next to Coco. Then came the night when he fell into a state of catatonic bliss as with an amiable grunt Coco acknowledged his presence by bestowing a few licks on the top of his head.

After that Meenie was no longer lonely. Wherever he went, usually in Coco's wake, he walked with confidence. He belonged. There had been born another one of those warm cat friendships that are not all that infrequent, if we only stop to observe.

Era Zistel

Revey

The Revenant

We called him Revey for short.

He was not particularly attractive, just an ordinary red tiger with a white shirt front and white shoes and a small smudge of red on his nose, as if the painter had cleaned off his brush there. But we had found a home for him. He was to go to a woman who owned a dairy farm and needed a barn cat. Her love for cats was close to equaling mine, so I knew she would be good to him.

But when she came to get him I couldn't find him. I searched and searched, she waited and waited, then couldn't wait any more, and we thought maybe we'd have to get used to having seventeen cats instead of sixteen. However, hours passed and still there was no sign of the little red and white kitten. Darkness came, and with it all the predators from the woods, foxes and wild cats and coyotes and owls and dogs that would make short work of such a little fellow. So we closed the door at the end of the day with sorrow, not liking to think of any animal, surplus or not, coming upon such a fate.

The next morning, to make sure, I telephoned neighbors up and down the road, asking if they had seen anything of a little red and white kitten. They had not. There was no trace of him anywhere then or for ten more days. Then on the eleventh day I went outside and tripped over something that skittered between my feet. It was the little red and white kitten, frisky as the sunlit morning, in fine condition, not even hungry, as substantiated by his turning down the milk hastily poured for him.

Where had he been, how had he lived, this helpless kitten, all those days he had been away? Again I questioned niehgbors. Not one had seen him. But now he was at home as if he'd never left, leading a normal life, eating baby food, drinking milk, making friends with Sonny, who was nearly the same age, playing kitten games with him. Then all at once he was gone again—and so was Sonny. Once more we searched and questioned neighbors, and closed the door at the end of the day with real sadness, for we had been very fond of Sonny, and the little red and white fellow had begun to steal into our hearts.

They were gone for five days. On the sixth I saw them trotting up the hill, coming from the woods in back of the house, both looking very fit and well fed and quite pleased with themselves and all of life.

This was the beginning of a firm friendship. The two of them played together, ate together, slept together—and disappeared together. They would stay home for a while, seemingly contented, having no intention of departing, and all at once they would be gone, and we would not see them for several days or a week or more.

It was after their second reappearance that we named the red and white kitten Revenant. "Something must have happened to him that first time," we said, half in jest, "and it is his indestructible ghost that returns to us now." But Sonny was no ghost, and he kept disappearing and reappearing in exactly the same way.

Once I happened to see them starting out. They walked side by side, confident, as if they knew precisely where they were going and were rather eager to get there. Even now their kitten legs had difficulty scrambling over boulders and fallen trees, for they were going into the densest part of the woods. I followed at a distance, as noiselessly as possible, with considerable anticipation, looking forward to solving the mystery of this other life of theirs.

They went to the foot of the hill a little over a quarter of a mile from the house, crossed a shallow brook by hopping from stone to stone with amusing kitten unsteadiness. Just beyond it they entered a thorny raspberry patch—and vanished. It was as if the earth had opened and swallowed them. One minute I saw them, the next they were gone, and although I hunted all around the berry patch, I could find no trace of them.

Ten days later they were back home again.

Once they were sufficiently grown so that I knew they could handle reasonably well the various challenges they'd encounter in the woods, I worried less about these periodic absences, even came to expect them. But one day Revey was home and Sonny was not, and I knew something had happened to him.

That was how we usually lost our cats. They'd go off in the morning and not come back in the evening, or ever again. Sometimes, by way of a witness, we'd find out what peril they had encountered, sometimes we would find them, or what was left of them, sometimes we could only surmise. With Sonny it was surmising. Tufts of his fur were scattered under a tree near the road, and a couple of poorly kept dogs had done much killing in the vicinity.

Revey called and cried and searched, then grew silent, and went away. This time he was gone for six months.

During this lengthy absence of his our house was rebuilt. A new section was added, a wall torn away, a room considerably enlarged. I often wondered what Revey would think about it when he returned, for even though so much time had elapsed I was sure he would. He was a revenant.

He came late at night, having adopted the ways of the wild, entered the house confidently, then stood transfixed, not believing what he saw. Where there had been a small room there was now a big one. He prowled around uneasily, picking up old scents but not trusting them, until he came to the place where the old wall had been. Beyond this he would not go. I tried to entice him into the new part of the room with food, the kind he liked especially, but he would not cross the imaginary boundary line. One side of the room was home, the other unknown and perhaps hostile territory. He never did enter it.

Shortly after his return this time I decided to try to tell the story of a cat's life in photos, a major undertaking. As a model I first chose the most photogenic of the cats, a handsome Persian named Ruff, but soon gave that up as hopeless. Ruff didn't mind having his picture taken, providng he was not disturbed. The story of his life became a series of somnolent poses and wide yawns. Other cats were eliminated for various reasons. Huckleberry was too lanky, Doody and Black Boy were camera shy, Melly and Sailor combatic and too frequently battle-scarred, the females too skittery. That left Revey, the ordinary red tiger. It wasn't until I saw the first photos of him that I realized he was beautiful.

As a model he surpassed perfection, seeming to sense what I wanted, sometimes even anticipating my wishes. We would go to a place I had chosen, with a small gesture I'd ask him to stay there, occasionally return after viewing him through the camera's eye to lift his head or shift his body a little, and he would remain still as a statue until he heard the click of the camera's shutter. Then he would dance with joy. He loved being photographed.

The only time we had trouble was when I tried to get a picture of him going away from me. Impossible. He simply couldn't figure out what I wanted, tried posing attractively here and there, went through a charming series of antics, and nothing seemed to please me. For what seemed like hours we just stood around, in the cold, in the snow, without his hearing a single click from the camera. Finally he must have said to himself, "I've had enough of this. I'm going home." Away he went and at last the shutter clicked. I got the picture of the cat walking away—so simple, but the hardest I ever took.

Some days the weather was bad. Revey would gaze out of the window and sulk and mope and finally start to cry, until with a sigh I agreed to go out and take a couple of pictures. It was not enough to merely point the camera at him. He had to hear the click. Once I did some clicking without any film in the camera, but felt so guilty I never did it again.

We went out in all kinds of weather, in fog and rain and snow, and the file marked "Revey" is full of useless pictures taken on inclement days. Through winter and spring and summer we worked together, and not once in all that time did he disappear. When autumn arrived I'd begun to feel something like a cat, and he must have felt quite a bit like a human. We were practically inseparable. Even at night he was at my side, occasionally waking to reach out to touch my cheek with his paw.

In October the book was almost finished. We had gone through all four seasons, the entire year. There were a few pictures I was not satisfied with and wanted to retake, but that would have to wait until after the hunting season. The only way we could insure the safety of the cats at this time was to keep them shut up. The females were confined in the house, the males in a large outdoor cage. Now Revey presented a problem. He would resent being shut up with the females, and also with the hoi-polloi in the big cage. He was special.

So I built a smaller cage that was his very own. Every day I would let him out of it for a little while. We would take a few turns around the house—the woods being out of bounds—and to please him I would take a few pictures. He was so good about returning to the cage, almost as if he understood why, that gradually the intervals of freedom lengthened.

That year had been unusually dry. All through summer and fall there had been no substantial rain. Deprived of life-giving moisture, the trees had shed their leaves earlier than usual. Day and night there was a pattering on the ground, like stealthy footfalls. They piled up all around the house, knee deep in spots, a fire hazard just when hunters might be throwing burning cigarettes out of car windows as they cruised along the roads.

All other activities had to be neglected to take care of this important one: raking leaves into piles and transporting them to a gully where they could be packed and watered down. There was no time for me to take pictures, I explained to Revey as I took him out of his cage.

"Tomorrow," I promised him. "Tomorrow the leaves will be gone and we can get back to normal. We'll take twice as many pictures."

The day was beautiful, the sky deep blue and cloudless, with a gentle, warm breeze blowing. Everywhere there was a brilliant color and the scent of dying that, in nature, is as good and clean as that of birth. Once in a while there were shots in the woods, but they were far away.

Revey played in the leaves, doing his best to attract my attention, then climbed a tree to pose among its branches, and when even that did not entice me he lay down on a patch of grass that had been raked clean, where he looked so contented, stretched out in lazy abandonment, that I felt reassured and had no misgivings about not putting him back in the cage.

Toward the end of the afternoon the sunlight shifted

away from his patch of grass and he moved to a rock nearby. The rays of the setting sun came through the trees to bathe him in dazzling light, and sitting in it, with the dark green of hemlocks behind him, he shone as if made of gold. It was a picture of such breathtaking beauty that I stood for a moment to memorize it, then thought of getting the camera to take just this one picture.

It didn't take long to carry away the last load of leaves. Then I dashed into the house, snatched up the camera, hurried out again, and saw only the bare rock. Revey was nowhere in sight.

"He can't have gone far," I told myself, and I called to him. "Look, I have the camera. Please go back on the rock. Let me take that one picture of you."

I looked around with confidence at first. He couldn't have gone far. But just as in those early days when he was only a kitten, the earth seemed to have opened up and swallowed him. Finally the circles I made through the woods grew too wide and darkness made it impossible for me to see. I had to return home with reproach nagging at my heels.

During the days that followed I did not dare call, for fear of luring him into the open just when a hunter was passing through. But in the nights that were so still you could hear a mouse scurrying along its runway, and a leaf falling to the ground was almost like a shout, I stood at the edge of the woods and pleaded with him to come home. Sometimes a bird would cry out in alarm, sometimes there would be quick footfalls through the dry leaves in the underbrush, but always going away, not coming to me.

When the first snow fell I went out at night and searched by flashlight. There were squirrel tracks and mouse tracks and bird tracks, the sharp indentation of deer hooves, the heavy imprints of a hunter's boots, but no cat tracks anywhere. Then near the end of the hunting season there was a heavier snow and I planned to go out and search again that night, even though it would be safe for Revey to travel during the day. It was cold. It was time for him to come home.

Early that afternoon a friend stopped by for a visit. He had been hunting in the woods nearby and had decided to call it a day. I gave him coffee and started looking for something for him to eat, but he said he didn't want anything, couldn't eat anything, and after a few sips of the coffee he told me why.

He had seen a cat in the woods.

I knew what that meant. I showed him Revey's book, and pushing aside the coffee cup he looked through it, at all the pictures taken in spring and summer and fall and winter that told the story of Revey's life.

"Wonderful," he said when he came to the end. "Wonderful."

Then with surprising vehemence for one who was himself a killer he slammed his hand down on the table.

"They shot the guts out of him."

So he was no revenant.

The man offered to take me there. It was not far. Revey had been on his way home and had almost made it. But I did not want a picture of horror superimposed on those others I had of him. Let him rest there in the woods,

I said. Let the snow that is falling give him cover, and when that snow melts in the spring, let the sexton beetles give him a decent burial.

Holding his book in my hands, I live again with him through that year we spent together, enjoying the birth of life in the spring, lazing through summer, romping in autumn leaves and winter snows. Then I close my eyes and see him in that final picture, the one that is not in the book, sitting in the slanting sunlight, gold against green, with the shots in the woods still far away.

[Editor's Note: Revey's book is *Wintertime Cat*, reprinted in 1988 by J. N. Townsend Publishing.]

The Cat That Could

He was my cat, but I didn't know him very well.

As a kitten he had been venturesome, the first one out of the box, the first to explore the house and go outside. That was why he was named Marco Polo, soon shortened to Marco, to which he responded, if he felt like it, with the slight twitch of an ear.

He became a cat, and spent most days roaming the woods at the back of our house. Sometimes I'd run into him there and it would be almost like two strangers meeting, with hardly more than a glance exchanged. But at the end of the day he always came home to eat and sleep, so at least to that extent he was my cat.

I'd probably not have missed him too much if one day he had failed to return, but something else happened. One day a car came speeding down the road. I heard a screech of brakes, a scream, and ran out to find Marco lying in the ditch, stretched out, head thrown back, eyes wide open, unseeing.

There was no sign of life.

I put him in a cardboard box, started looking for tools to dig a grave, then heard a faint moan. He was not dead, not quite.

I took care of him as best I could, nursed him until he was on his feet again, fully recovered—or so I thought. Until then he had been just one of the cats, not particularly favored, so maybe that was why I never noticed that we no longer met in the woods or that he, the bold one, had become oddly timid and withdrawn.

The next day when we were both outside I was struck by his peculiar gait, a stiff, cautious lope, each paw raised high, thrust forward slowly. Hasty examination revealed nothing wrong that I could detect, but forsaking his customary aloofness he nervously sinuated against my hand as if trying to tell me of some great need. Then as I made an abrupt movement he flinched and ran—and crashed headlong into a basket left lying in the path.

He was blind.

How long had he been feeling his way like that, as a blind person taps and searches with a cane? How often had he gone hungry because he could not get past the unseen hostility of the other cats to reach the food—or didn't even know the food was there?

I had believed cats were gifted with a keen sense of smell, but when given food on a separate plate he never knew it was there until he walked into it. That remained an upsetting problem quite literally, until I thought of tapping on the floor, a signal he quickly learned meant food had been put precisely there.

I hovered over him, snatched objects out of his way,

made sure furniture was not moved and nothing was left
lying about, until I realized I was doing him no favor. He
was still an explorer. Nothing gave him greater pleasure
than discovering something out of place. So I turned about
and made changes deliberately to add zest to his restricted
life.

When he started climbing trees it didn't bother me
too much, but the first time I saw him on the roof, serenely
sunning himself, my heart skipped a beat. In panic I tried
to think how he might be rescued, then saw there was no
need. Evidently sensing my presence down below, he got
up, yawned, stretched, and walked to the edge of the roof,
the very edge. There was a branch about a foot away. He
waved a paw to locate it, tapped to make certain, then
leaped onto it, walked along the branch to the trunk of the
tree, shinnied down and nonchalantly ambled over to me.

As his assurance increased, so did his wandering.
While he still could see he must have often visited a pond
some five hundred feet down the road and an equal
distance back in the woods. Now I began getting telephone
calls, or neighborhood children would come to tell me,
"Marco's down at the pond." That seemed impossible but
I'd go there and call, and from somewhere in the brush
he'd answer, and we'd keep up the exchange until I located
him. Then he'd ride back home on my shoulder, never
doubting my ability to protect him if a car roared past.

Once in a while I'd catch him starting out, trotting
briskly, keeping well to the side of the road. Then I had
only to speak sharply and he'd turn around to march back
home again. He knew that I didn't like his going to the

Marco

pond. Yet he'd sneak away whenever he could.

If instead he went to the woods behind the house he was fairly safe. Just as in the past, I'd sometimes come across him there, and would watch in amazement as he threaded his way among the trees without ever quite bumping into anything. Like some blind people, he seemed to have a kind of radar that warned him of obstacles just ahead.

Occasionally he did get lost, when the barking of a dog or some other menacing sound made him run in panic, flopping like a fish out of water, paying no attention to direction. Then he needed me. Sending out a cry that I came to recognize as a call for help, he would listen for my reply, flounder toward it, touch against my leg, then walk beside me, like a heeling dog, until the way became familiar again.

At first his blind bumbling had infuriated the other cats. Collisions with them were unavoidable and he would be cuffed, usually across the vulnerable eyes that did not know when to close. A big male named Pert was particularly hostile and gave him many an unwarranted beating.

Then something strange happened. For days Pert stared at Marco with a puzzled expression in his eyes. He could not have concluded that Marco was blind, but somehow he must have realized that allowances ought to be made. Whenever he saw Marco heading toward him he quickly stepped to one side. Later the other cats seemed to arrive at a similar understanding, and Marco walked in peace.

Years passed. All of us became so used to Marco's infirmity that we took it for granted, and maybe, as memory dimmed, he too took it for granted. Until his tenth year he continued making trips to the pond, and almost daily one of my chores was to call for him there. Then the pond was drained, the trees were cut, the land was turned into a campsite. That ended his visits there. Instead he went to the woods behind the house. At the end of the day I'd go to meet him there, and we'd walk home together, he digressing a bit now and then to climb a tree and walk tightrope along a branch while I watched with misgivings, or pursue windblown leaves in clumsy gallops that made me laugh and want to cry.

When he was twelve there were signs of decline. He no longer sunned himself on the roof, seldom climbed trees, stopped going into the woods, seemed content to just lie in a patch of sunlight near the house.

Then when he was thirteen he had a stroke. In the middle of the night I was awakened by a terrible commotion and found him writhing on the floor, unable to get to his feet.

I made him a bed in a box, once again took care of his needs as best I could, and I debated. Putting him to sleep meant taking him to the vet, subjecting him to unseen terror, strange noises, strange smells, strange hands—unless I did the job myself. I tried to find the courage, and discovered there was no need. Marco himself had no intention of giving up.

Day after day he worked on the paralyzed legs, moving them no more than a twitch at first, then a little more, a little more until he could draw them up under his body. He tried to stand and fell, tried again and fell, kept on trying until at last he was on his feet, swaying, triumphant.

When he tried to walk the legs dragged, giving him a peculiar undulating gait. Every so often he'd flop over, but he was determined. Asking to be let outside, he tumbled down the steps, picked himself up and went to where he had made up his mind to go, in his favorite patch of sunlight.

Early in his fifteenth year he had another stroke, a minor one that had no lasting effect, except for some weakness of the sphincter muscles. He always had been scrupulously clean, preferring to use the earth out of doors, where he scratched and sniffed and scratched until sure his deposit had been well covered. So this new disability was most distressing. Whenever I heard him hiss at himself I knew he'd had another accident.

Then came a marked change in his behavior. He grew restless, could hardly wait to get outside each morning, but instead of lying in the sun he looked toward the woods and howled.

That's the way it is with many animals. Feeling the end of life approaching, they want to visit for a last time the places they loved in their youth. Marco wanted to go back to the woods, but couldn't, by himself.

I enjoyed the woods too, so each afternoon I'd call, "You want to go for a walk?" and he'd come flopping over to join me.

Crossing the brook was a problem. I tried carrying him, but he wriggled impatiently, wanting to walk, to be independent even though he couldn't find the stepping stones. Finally I thought of the tapping signal, and slapped my foot down on each stone so he could follow the sound. That worked quite well, although sometimes he lost his footing and fell in anyway. No matter. He clawed his way back onto the stone, shook himself, regained his balance, and plodded on.

We went everywhere, he wandering free, sometimes out of sight, yet keeping close track of my whereabouts, for the moment he heard me starting home he'd hurry to catch up.

Over the years he had grown sensitive not only to my tone of voice, but also to my moods. When I was out of sorts he knew it, and moped. When I was in a good mood he knew that, too, and my occasional singing, which even made me wince, so delighted him that he'd respond with a burst of gaiety, tumbling about in dreadful imitation of a playful kitten.

Once when he was quite far away a fox barked in a thicket. The sound meant nothing to him, suggested no danger, but fear made my voice sharp and he reacted with alarm, scrambling and falling every which way to reach safety at my side.

My wish was that the end would come for him there in the woods where he most wanted to be, but that was not granted.

He is still with us.

His world has now become very small, not much bigger than an upturned box near the heater in the kitchen. But on warmer days, when the sun is shining—even indoors, in his darkness, he knows if the sun is shining— he goes out to sit on the top step, turning his head this and that way as though looking at things, actually listening to small sounds, the flight of a bird, perhaps, or an insect rustling in the dry leaves. His hearing has remained acute.

As he sits there waiting for the end I give him not my pity—he would dislike that as much as being carried across the brook—but my gratitude. He has shown me how to face adversity, and how to bear it with courage.

The Little Ghost

It is possible that my attitude toward cats is not quite normal. We usually have too many. Even so, people seem to think we don't have enough, because each fall vacationers leave batches of them as parting gifts in our driveway or somewhere in the immediate vicinity.

They are of all sizes, colors, ages, but have one thing in common. They are hungry. It seems cruel to send them off on a journey on an empty stomach, so we give them a good feed, then at considerable expense, take them to the vet for that final trip.

But there was one once—

A cardboard box lay in the ditch at the side of the road that morning, quite late in the fall of the year. Since our summer visitors often throw rubbish out of their cars in such boxes, we have learned not to be curious about their contents. This one stayed in the ditch all day, ignored.

Toward evening some rain fell. Then that night the temperature went down, until when we went to bed it was close to twenty. The next morning there was some snow on the ground, and frozen leaves crackled underfoot. The box was still in the ditch. Then a neighbor who had walked up the road to pay us a visit called out to us.

"Come see what's in this box."

He has a better stomach than mine, I thought, but I went out to peer through the opening he had torn in the sodden cardboard. Inside the box were a soggy blanket, a bone crawling with maggots, and a kitten.

A shivering, silent white ghost of a kitten gazing up at us with the most startling blue eyes I had ever seen, like sapphires set in a wisp of cloud.

I took her into the house and prepared to take her on the final trip, but the roads were bad, and besides, she would not eat. Two days and a night in the ditch, exposed to the rain, the sudden freeze, had been too much for her tiny body to withstand. Each time she inhaled there was a crackling in her chest like that of the frozen leaves. A discharge had hardened into crusts around her nostrils. She was very ill.

She lapped up some water but turned away from the food I offered. How could I send her away on a long trip like that? All the others had had full bellies and had been content to curl up for their final sleep. Besides, I could not bear closing the lids over the vividness of those blue eyes.

I could not leave her in the house because the other cats were hostile toward her, and she'd already been subjected to too much terror. In the cage often used as temporary shelter for baby rabbits or squirrels or chipmunks or birds or whatever else came my way, I gave her a warm blanket, and I put the cage in the tool shed. She accepted the comfort of the blanket with a crackling sigh. Then, after I had washed her eyes and nostrils and stroked her for a while, there was above the noisy breathing another sound. She purred.

Late that night a fox barked near the road. The next morning the cardboard box with the soggy blanket and the maggoty bone was gone. At least she had been spared that terror.

She was so like a wraith that I called her Little Ghost. Bedded down in a box placed in a patch of sunlight where she could watch me, she went everywhere with me that day while I worked outside.

The crackling in her chest was worse. I could see how she fought for each breath. Yet whenever I spoke to her or touched her, the little instrument in her throat began to grind out a melody. She was close to death, but she was happy. She had a fine soft warm bed to die on, and what more can a humble little kitten ask for in this world of pain and sorrow?

But the warm sunlight was life's ally, death's foe. When toward evening I put her back in the cage she seemed to breathe more easily. Now the purring was louder than the crackling. She still would eat no solid food, but did lap up a saucer of milk. Again I bathed her eyes and nostrils and stayed with her for a while, giving her the palm of my hand as a pillow for her head until, with a long, shuddering sigh, the purring stopped and she slept.

The next morning brought another fine day, the sun traveling in a cloudless sky. I put Little Ghost in her blanket-lined box and carried her outside again, to move her about as the sunlight moved. Each time I shifted the box she gazed up at me gratefully, and her whole frail body shook with the purring.

Late in the afternoon she took a small portion of meat from my hand, and that evening, after she had been put back in her cage, she ate a bit more and drank some milk. It began to look as though she might live after all, and even though she was only a stray, and one too many if I kept her, it seemed most important to me that she should.

The next morning she ate willingly, not much, but enough to keep her alive. Again the sky was cloudless. She still had to be carried in the box to follow the healing sunlight, but in the afternoon she sat up and tried to wash her bedraggled fur. When she licked a paw with a pale tongue and passed it over the back of an ear I was almost certain she would recover.

I had forgotten what a fickle ally the sun could be.

That night the wind shifted and came from the east. The stars winked out, the sky blackened, the trees whispered, the air smelled of rain. I went out to Little Ghost and put a blanket over her cage and moved it farther back into the shed. When I talked to her she sat up and rubbed her head against my hand, and she purred. The crackling in her chest was almost gone.

All that night there was a soft pattering of rain on the roof, a pleasant, cozy sound if no death lurks in the vicinity. The morning was grey and cold, with occasional heavy downpours of rain, and Little Ghost was worse. The crackling in her chest was back. But she ate, and drank some milk. There still might have been hope if only, somewhere in that dreary day, there had been somewhere a small patch of sunlight.

I tried bringing her into the house again and had to take her out because the other cats terrified her. Back in the shed she lay quietly in her cage all day, accepting what now seemed inevitable. Toward evening the tips of her ears and her legs grew cold. Curled up in a soft ball of tousled fur she seemed to sleep, and when I stroked her made no response but one. She purred.

During the night the rain stopped. The sky cleared. There will be sun tomorrow, I thought, healing sun for her to lie in. I went out to visit her one more time before going to bed.

The small body was still curled up in sleep, but it was cold. The Little Ghost was dead.

No, not quite. Not quite. From the cold body came a sound in response to the touch of my hand, an echo of an echo of a sound. The tiny instrument in the dead throat purred.

I buried her in the graveyard where she did not rightly belong. She was not an old friend. But somehow I could not put her in the Potter's Field in the woods where all the other unknowns lie.

You see, I am not quite normal.

Squeak

The Saga of Squeak

Lately I've been making trips to what we call the woodlot, a stand of old hemlocks and beeches in back of the house. The reason for those visits goes back a few years, to an afternoon when I happened to glance out of the window at the wrong moment.

There was a stray cat in the yard, a scruffy-looking grey tiger, limping slightly because a part of one paw was missing. What followed was routine: food put on a plate, the plate carried out and put down about where the stray had been before fleeing at the sight of me. After I'd gone back into the house he returned, sniffed suspiciously and devoured the food.

Precisely according to routine, the next day he was back, and the day after that he limped over to meet me. But there, as far as I was concerned, routine ended. No friendship this time. He'd get food from me, and that was all.

So I never spoke to him or even looked at him except out of the corner of my eye. But when he was not immediately within range of the corner of my eye, I'd make some comment to myself, like, "Well, where is he?" And one day he answered with a rusty sounding squeak.

That's how he got his name. And as everyone knows, once you've given an animal a name, you're hooked. Instead of mumbling to myself I began calling, "Hi, Squeak." Then I stood by while he ate, and going a step farther, patted him on the head and, finally, in a weak moment, even invited him into the house.

Fortunately he had the good sense to refuse, evidently looking upon houses as huge traps, which in a way they are, and preferring to retire to the house he already had, a mound of hay in an abandoned barn. So our relationship remained satisfactorily tenuous. His only obligation was to appear and eat, mine to provide the sustenance. But something always has to spoil perfect arrangements like that. One day he ran in terror as a neighbor's dogs lunged into the yard to wolf down his dinner.

After pondering for about half an hour, I looked for lumber and built a shelf outside our kitchen window. There, out of reach of the dogs, Squeak could eat in peace. What I hadn't planned on was that he could also peer through the window, and next to eating this became his favorite occupation. By the hour he squatted on the shelf, watching all the goings and comings in the kitchen, always rising to pay proper homage when I passed by, which was so disconcerting that I began making detours to stay out of sight.

Almost every animal lays claim to a territory of some kind. Larger animals may "own" a square mile or more, small ones only a field, or a plot of just a few square yards.

The shelf became Squeak's territory. No one else was allowed to set foot on it—except the birds.

One day I was astonished to see a flock of chickadees had joined him to share his dinner. They pecked on one side of the plate while he ate on the other. If one became overbold and fluttered too close around his head he raised a paw to give it an impatient swat. Otherwise he paid little attention.

What was the matter with him? Didn't he know he was a cat?

All through the winter the chickadees ate with him. Then with the arrival of spring they departed for the woods and more normal fare, but in the fall they were back, and with them an observant squirrel sometimes darted in to grab a bite or two. Finally I got so used to seeing this strange assemblage outside the window that it no longer seemed strange.

Early in Squeak's third summer of our acquaintance I decided to clean up the pasture, an acre of open field down a hill a few hundred feet from the house. Every afternoon I'd spend perhaps an hour cutting brush and picking up fallen branches, and after a while I noticed that I was never alone. Squeak was there, too, not exactly with me, but somewhere in the vicinity.

Then I noticed that when I walked down the hill he was also walking down the hill, again not exactly with me but going in the same direction. And finally he was sitting in the path each afternoon waiting for me. Once I played a mean trick on him, gave him his dinner and immediately started down the hill for the pasture. He left his dinner and caught up with me.

An eminently successful businessman I once knew had a hard and fast rule. Telephone calls would be accepted and appointments made only before and after his favorite soap opera. Now, to the amusement of some friends and the annoyance of others, whatever plans I made had to be either before or after Squeak. When all the branches and brush had been stacked in neat piles and there was really nothing more to do in the pasture, I went there anyway and sat on a flat rock to gaze at the green treetops and the blue sky, enjoying just doing nothing for a while, and Squeak sat nearby, gazing up at me.

Winter finally put an end to those pilgrimages. I had no inclination to trek through the snow to the pasture, and Squeak seemed to agree. He went back to window watching. And once the habit was broken, I was determined that it should stay that way. When he started sitting on the path the following summer I pretended not to notice, and after a couple of weeks he gave up waiting for me.

But then, early in the fall, along came the fuel shortage. Like a lot of other people I acquired a wood stove, which necessitated my going into the woodlot every day to cut up fallen branches and trees, and of course I had company.

No matter how unpleasant the weather, Squeak had to go along. When winter snows piled up, I broke trail, he followed. Wherever I chose to do my sawing, he sat hunched on a rock or a stump jutting above the snow, and if he couldn't find one or the other close by he simply sat on the snow. So I found a burlap bag that I could carry along and put down for him to sit on.

Now the fuel shortage is over and the weather's warm and there's no longer need for me to go to the woodlot to do all that sawing. But I'm going anyway, because there's Squeak waiting, half rising whenever I walk by, thinking maybe this time I'll pick up the saw and his burlap bag and head in the right direction. So once again, like the businessman with his soap opera, I am making appointments before and after half an hour or so with a cat.

There ought to be a way to avoid such entanglements. Next time I see a stray in the yard....

The Boob

She appeared in our back yard shortly before Christmas.

I have a weakness for cats, so of course I didn't want her. If you have a weakness for cats you already have too many.

Out of the corner of my eye I saw that she was black and scrawny, with sparse dull fur and a skinny rat tail. I didn't want to really look at her for fear she'd see the weakness in me and try to take advantage of it. If I ignored her, I thought, she'd get discouraged and go away, either back where she came from or somewhere else. But at the end of the day she was still around.

The next day I indulged my weakness to the extent of putting out a plate of food for her. Not food especially made, just a plate of leftovers my cats had rejected. I did not speak to her, did not look at her. I simply put the plate down and walked away.

She didn't go to it immediately, but an hour later I noticed the food was gone. Whether she or someone else had eaten it I didn't know—and didn't care, I told myself perhaps a bit too belligerently.

My own cats were also belligerent. Once they discovered she wouldn't fight back they really got going on her, even the females not fully grown. Of course it would have been much more fun if she had run from them and they could have given her a good chase through the woods, but even so it was rather a fine game making her dart under the rabbit cage. Soon a regular path was worn there, from her frequent comings and goings. Apparently she also spent her nights under the cage, because once when she wasn't around I looked, and saw a round nest pressed in the hay that had fallen down from the cage.

I continued putting food out for her each evening and except for that ignored her; and I suppose it might have worked out all right that way if the weather had cooperated. One night the mercury plummeted, and stayed down around the zero mark for the next five days. To make conditions worse it snowed, and it blew, and the wind carried the snow under the rabbit cage.

I told myself it would warm up soon, that she would get through this cold spell somehow, that fourteen cats were more than enough, that she wasn't pretty anyway. But when I couldn't avoid glancing at her I could see how she was shivering. I wondered, too, what she was doing for water, with the ground frozen fast and the brook covered with ice and snow. Eating the snow, I told myself. That's what wild animals do.

Nevertheless, one night when the wind blew harder than ever, driving still more snow under the rabbit cage, I stood before it and said, "Oh, all right. Come on, then." Toward these words so grudgingly spoken the miserable black creature came instantly, to creep into my arms. I carried her into the house, past the outraged glare of the resident cats, put her in the bedroom and closed the door.

It wasn't long before the bona fide members of the household turned the intrusion into a diversion. Lining up before the bedroom door, they snuffled along the crack under it and spat taunts, daring the other to come out and face them.

Half an hour later, when I chased them away and went in to look at her, I found her sitting on the lower corner of the bed, still shivering, but washing herself ardently, and purring. I said, somewhat idiotically, "Boo!" and she answered with a disarming little "Prrrt?" Now that I looked at her, really looked for the first time, I saw that she had one redeeming feature. Her eyes, large, round, vivid green in the black setting, were of such compelling depth that, having looked into them, you noticed nothing else. The thin face, the gaunt body, the straggly fur didn't matter. She had that extraordinary beauty, in those eyes.

For five days she stayed on the lower corner of the bed. This had become her home. Three times a day I carried her outside to allow her to make her contribution to the earth's fertility and get chased under the rabbit cage. I'd wait for a while, call to her, snatch her safely away from a menacing onslaught, take her back into the bedroom, put her on the lower corner of the bed, and close the door. That was her life, except for the little game we played. Whenever I opened the door I'd say, "Boo!" and she'd answer,

"Prrrt?" So she came to be known as Boo, although that was soon changed to Boob. Without doubt she was the most stupid, unenterprising cat I'd ever encountered.

Remaining entirely inactive seemed to satisfy her completely. Except for the washing, which was her only and almost constant occupation, she did nothing but sit quietly on the bed, and might have continued to do that indefinitely, I suppose, if I hadn't decreed otherwise. As long as she had become a member of our family I thought she should join it, thus freeing me from the extra chore of fixing an extra plate for her, filling another bowl with water, and carrying her outside. On the sixth day I opened the bedroom door.

The other cats immediately rushed in, took possession of the room, but to their credit granted her squatter's rights. Just as they had not invaded her sanctuary under the rabbit cage, so now they did not try to chase her off the corner of the bed. That was hers, little though it might be.

After the door had been open a few days she made a first timid attempt at exploration. She hopped down from the bed and stood in the doorway. The others granted her this right also, but every once in a while, in passing, reached out to clout her, just for the fun of it. She never retaliated, only winced and sometimes, if the blow was a hard one, cried out. But she kept right on standing there.

That's when I became aware of how really stupid she was. In size she was a match for any one of them. If she had hit back she'd soon have put them off, and I'd have been spared the trouble of running to her rescue, too often a thankless task, because even in this respect she was dull-witted. I had been good to her, fed her well, tended her needs, shown her every kindness. Yet sometimes when I approached her she would wince as if she expected to be struck by me, too, and if we happened to be outside, dodge and run away. This was particularly annoying if it was raining and I had bent down to pick her up.

There was also her inability to comprehend the swinging door. It worked quite easily, either way. In varying lengths of time all the others had learned to use it, so, to our distraction, had various wild animals from the woods. But Boo? No. I put her through to show her how it operated and she clutched at me in terror, as if she expected to fall at least seventeen stories on the other side. I held it open for her so she could see it was a means of entrance. She stared at me amiably with those big beautiful vacant eyes and waited for me to pick her up. Then like as not when I tried, she would suddenly take fright and run away.

After a long, long time she did come to understand there was a way she could get in or out, but the exact procedure still eluded her. She would try to push against the whole door, or the wrong panel. By luck she sometimes found the right one, but such experience did not add up to knowledge.

She also had an odd way with food. No matter how hungry she was, when I put down her plate of food she would not go to it at once, but waited until some time after I had left the room to go and eat, as if this were a prohibited action that had to be indulged in furtively.

A strange, muddle-headed creature she was, with us

yet not one of us, like a not very well known guest paying a visit. Although I fed her and cared for her and carried her around, I could not say I had any special regard for her.

Then one bright sunny day I was looking out of the window as she crossed the yard, not really watching her, but she happened to be in my line of vision, and because she was I saw her walk straight into a tree.

Oh, I was the stupid one, not she! She was blind, and I had been too blind to notice. Now comprehension flooded in. Her slowness to join the family had not been timidity. Her unwillingness to fight back had not been cowardice. Her inability to use the swinging door had not been incomprehension. She had not gone to her food immediately because she hadn't known it was there. She had run from me when I tried to pick her up because I had neglected to speak to her first, and my footfall might have been menacing or not. She didn't know, and fled.

Now I saw how clever she was, lifting her feet high, as I had learned to do in the dark, putting each pad down carefully, testing the ground for unevenness or obstacles, so that almost never did she run into anything as she had on that day when I saw her bump into the tree. She had kept me in the dark for a long time. But now that I was aware of her darkness, there was a difference in her life.

I carried her out of doors, as I had done in the beginning. No more did she have to fear falling down on the other side of the swinging door. Whenever she started feeling her way cautiously across a room I cleared a path through the other cats, so that soon they came to know that in some way she was special, and must not be teased.

When I served her dinner I let her first smell the food, and always put the water bowl down in the same spot. And I tried to take care not to move the furniture about too much.

This last made her a bit overconfident. Small chairs do have a way of wandering, and sometimes, in supreme trust, she would leap upon one that wasn't there. Then the startled parabola she described in the air was a very funny and terrible thing to see. I, too, moved about. Frequently she would bump into me but at once, with a gesture of grace, this mishap was converted into a caress against my leg.

Outside, beyond my surveillance, she got along well enough. Now that I kept an eye on her I noticed she had by trial and error paced out a safe route to travel. She would start where I had put her down at the foot of the steps, cross the yard, turn to the right when she came to a certain boulder, go toward a large hemlock at the edge of the woods and, amazingly, climb it to the first limb. Then, having carefully lowered herself to the ground, she would circle the tree, go through a patch of ferns marked by a line of brown from her daily passage, then disappear in the woods. She would not be gone long, no more than fifteen or twenty minutes, and always reappeared at exactly the same spot just behind the rabbit cage under which she had once lived. She would stop for a moment at the entrance to this old residence, perhaps recalling the misery she had known then, and from it would go to the back door, follow the side of the house until she reached the front steps. There I picked her up and carried her indoors. There was never any variation, and every step of her path was known to me, except for that small part of it that went through the woods.

Then in October, about halfway along that path, where it went through the woods, the end came. Did she look like a rabbit?

I don't suppose the hunter wasted much pity on her. She could not have looked like much, lying bony flat, mouth open in surprise at this thing she had seen in her night, unless he stopped to examine her more closely and saw the beauty of those sightless eyes. Going from one darkness to another could not have changed them, not so soon, anyway.

A Gathering of Cats

Huckleberry is not very bright. Instead of pausing to take stock of the weather, the temperature or any overnight changes in the landscape, he plunges out the moment the door is opened and doesn't stop until he runs into a snowdrift or, in the absence of a snowdrift, until he reaches the brook. Even then sometimes he doesn't stop in time. Looking out of the window one morning I am puzzled and distressed to see him whirling around and around in mad circles, his tail stuck straight out behind him like a spear. Has he gone totally mad?

No, this is just one of the times when he hasn't stopped at the edge of the brook but plunged into it. Now, with the temperature well below freezing, he has icicles hanging from his belly and his tail has frozen stiff behind him. That's why he is going around in circles, trying to catch hold of the tail as a racehound would a fleeing hare. Each time he turns it swings out of sight. He is most grateful when I carry him in and place him beside the stove to thaw out. Of course, such a simple solution had not entered his addled head.

❧❧❧❧

Quagga has no great beauty, but the distinction of being just about the most ill-tempered cat one could find. Only a single love does she have, for the one being she believes she owns. Every evening, no matter what the weather, rain, snow, fierce wind, bitter cold, she must travel down the road to wait for me, huddled in the shallow ditch between the terror of the woods and the menace of the highway, so that she can escort me home.

She was a fierce and devoted mother, an implacable enemy of all other cats, so that I wonder how the kittens came into being. Now she has only one eye, the other having been lost in a fight. She is far from attractive, but for eight years she has been my devoted companion and I respect her, for her indomitable courage and her uncompromising tyranny.

❧❧❧❧

Amiable Black Boy was taken ill just when a snowstorm was raging. It was a long, hard drive. When we arrived at the vet's it was night, and we found only the woman at the desk and the vet's new partner, a young fellow, assured, who told us there was nothing to worry about, just a stone in the bladder. He'd have Black Boy as good as new in no time. Somehow I was filled with foreboding. I wanted to put Black Boy back into the carrier, get out of there. But he was ill. There was no place else to take him.

The young vet said an anesthetic would not be necessary but I insisted on it, and a good thing that was. In no time bungling attempts to insert a catheter had reduced the penis to a bloody pulp. The vet, grown stubborn, sweat rolling down his face, lips drawn back from clenched teeth, kept on trying, his clumsy fingers becoming even more brutal because he knew his efforts were useless. Finally, under pressure from his hands, the bladder broke. Black Boy woke up screaming in agony, writhing, and all I could think of was to shout, "Put him to death, quickly!" Then while he stood in a helpless daze, the woman and I carried the screaming cat to the gas chamber and put him in.

That was the merciful end for Black Boy, but not for me. All night long I lived through it again and again, the horror of seeing those terrible hands reduce living flesh to pulp. Yes, I knew that if we had kept Black Boy at home he would have had a miserable death. I knew that even a competent vet might not have been able to save him. But—

Had I been the genteel lady I am not, I'd have stayed in the waiting room instead of insisting on going along with Black Boy. Then the miserable fellow would have had time to recover his swaggering composure, to wipe the sweat off his face and wash the blood off his hands and comb back his hair, to make an assured entrance into the waiting room to tell me, with a proper amount of sympathy, that in spite of his very best efforts, Black Boy had expired.

And I'd never have known. I'd have thought, well, he seems a nice young fellow, and I'd have grieved over Black Boy but would not have gone through a night of horror. And very likely I'd have entrusted the other animals to his care and treatment. Now I know that I must do what I can with my own two hands, and if that is not enough for life, then these hands must give death.

❦❦❦❦

Along with her other lack of virtues, the effervescent Kate has a major shortcoming. She is crazy.

Well, not crazy, really, just harmlessly, pathetically, and most charmingly addle-pated.

A cat of three years going on four should know what motherhood is all about, but it always takes Kate completely by surprise, usually between a hop and a skip. And by the time the idea has entered her delicate eggshell head that things are not as they were or, in her opinion, ought to be, the kittens have departed, to await the call of a more suitable mother.

Once in a while, though, one manages to squeak through, and a thoroughly flustered Kate goes completely to pieces. What is this little thing, and what is she supposed to do with it? In a flurry of activity she really does nothing at all, beneficial, that is. The kitten is transported here and there, crooned over and rolled around by a tenderly administering tongue, then, having done all she could and raised it to the best of her ability, she goes off to take care of other matters.

I put the little thing to bed, and when I think it's time to feed it I go in search of Kate. In the garden she is happily flitting around like a butterfly, chasing a butterfly. I spend some time trying to catch the wisp of fur that she is, and carry her into the house.

Shown the kitten, she cries, "Oh my goodness, I forgot all about it! Oh, isn't it precious, isn't it adorable, isn't it positively divine?"

Later, when she finally is convinced that the kitten

is—although she certainly doesn't see why—her responsibility, she tucks it away for safekeeping, then can't remember where.

"I seem to have lost my kitten," she says to me. "Really, it must be around here somewhere. Would you have any idea where?"

So I have to abandon less important pursuits, like getting dinner, to go grubbing around under the bed, in the clothes closet, behind the refrigerator and in other less likely places, until the little thing is found.

"Oh, the poor sweet darling!" she croons over it. "My precious one!" She snuggles down with it to stay perhaps as much as half an hour, providing, that is, I stay with her.

Then she is outside again, hopping after grasshoppers or leaping over frogs.

Poor scatterbrained Kate! Sometimes I think I ought to feel sorry for her. But she doesn't feel sorry for herself. She hasn't even enough sense for that.

🐾🐾🐾🐾

Cleo was our first cat. We were living in the city then, in an apartment on the second floor.

One day I looked out the window and saw her in the courtyard below, scrawny, grimy, dusty-white creature with a distended belly and a nervously twitching tail. At the same moment I looked down she looked up. And that settled that, because I made the mistake of saying hello, and of course it took her no time at all to discover there was a fire escape leading from where she stood to where I was, enabling her to accept the invitation she thought she heard in that "hello."

Rung by rung she made the perilous ascent, to appear on the other side of the glass with her mouth open in a soundless hello of her own. It was only necessary for me to open the window.

So, just like that, we had a cat. Three days later Cleo's belly was reduced in size and we had three cats.

Once Cleo was smaller in that area and suitably filled out in others, she turned out to be a fairly handsome cat who did a pretty little dance following the plate of food from the serving counter to her corner. She was also a devoted mother, had, in fact, only one fault. She seemed to have been incorrigibly housebroken. Twice a day or bust, she had to make the hazardous trip down the fire escape, rung by rung, then back up again. Sometimes after a storm the rungs would be coated with ice, or piled high with snow that fell away dangerously under her feet. I would stand at the window holding my breath while she dug and squatted and scratched down below and made her way up.

We gave her a box filled in succession with paper, litter, sawdust, shavings, hard-to-come-by earth. She sat in it dutifully as long as we wished her to, looking virtuous but unhappy, never once considering this a substitute for the courtyard.

When the kittens were old enough we put them in the box, and it took them no time at all to learn that they could please us by making their little deposits there. Watching the kittens misbehave and get away with it, Cleo was at first greatly distressed, then puzzled, then speculative.

On one particularly stormy evening, with a gale wind

driving snow almost horizontally through the courtyard, she went to the window, asked to have it opened, stood in it gazing into the wild night, then turned and walked resolutely to the litter box. Before it she remained for some time staring at it, then in sudden decision stepped into it and squatted, and into her eyes there came a most blissful expression. This was luxury. This was bliss!

Cleo

Of all the cats I have known, there was one who liked to go swimming. Speck was her name. Gleaming black she was, with a white vest and little white shoes. The moment she heard the water running she would come galloping to plunge into the tub, to swim from end to end and back and forth, like a contestant in a swimming pool, making the turns with a flourish. She was the one who always went walking with me, on a leash, putting her diminutive feet down with pride, holding her head high, knowing she was attracting attention and enjoying it. Almost every day we met in a busy street an immense Russian wolfhound, and they became good friends. While they stood together, the great white dog lowering his massive head to touch noses with the dainty little cat, a crowd would gather to marvel. Then she would accompany me into the restaurant, and while I ate my dinner she would lie quietly under the table, to wait patiently until it was time to take me home.

She was killed at the pound. Someone had telephoned in a complaint about a stray black and white cat in the neighborhood. She was black and white. By chance she got into the courtyard on that day. She was friendly, easy to catch. As soon as I learned what had happened I telephoned frantically, hoping to save her, only to hear a polite, automatically sympathetic voice tell me that it was too late, she'd already been destroyed.

The unwanted black and white stray continued to prowl the neighborhood.

Moire

She was beautiful, a black and grey tabby with perfect watersilk markings, so she was named Moire. She was perfect in disposition, too, and that worried me. Perfection is not supposed to exist in this imperfect world. Let it be noticed, I thought, and she will be taken away.

So she almost was. When she was only a year old, suddenly she became very ill. The little brown nose was all at once hot and dry, her breathing became swift, and with each breath a noise like crumpled paper sounded in her chest. The veterinarian diagnosed viral pneumonia and gave no assurance that she would live.

I didn't want her to die abandoned and frightened in the hospital. I knew that those even less ill than she could die of no more than homesickness. So I told the veterinarian I would take her home and care for her myself. He shook his head, but gave me the necessary medication.

Day and night I nursed her, setting the alarm clock for her hourly doses of medicine, keeping her box at the foot of my bed so that I could watch over her.

Moire

It was difficult for both of us, but she did not fight against taking the medicine, seeming to realize that it was good for her. Once the administration became routine she would watch me approaching with a pill and actually open her mouth for me to drop it in, as if knowing this would relieve the cough and the pain in her chest.

However, the cough was sometimes found useful. She didn't mind the beef broth given to her with the medicine dropper but couldn't abide the eggnog. The moment the taste of it was on her tongue she started coughing, and kept on coughing until the obnoxious eggnog was removed, the beef broth substituted.

The crisis in her illness came in the middle of the night. Suddenly she raised her head and looked around wildly, as if the whole room had been invaded by things that leaped and flew all around her. Before I could stop her she had jumped out of the box and off the bed, to stagger swiftly across the floor as if chasing something, and in the middle of the room she fell on her side, to lie gasping.

I covered her with a blanket, not daring to lift her to put her back in the box. The thread of her life was too thin. With the blanket over her and my hand under her head she lay with the rattle in her chest growing louder and louder, faster and faster, until the terrible sound seemed to fill the entire room and make it hard for me to breathe. Her fever bright eyes looked up at me, terror in them. She was facing death, and she was afraid. The wild eyes appealed to me, "Please, let me stay!"

I sat beside her for a long time, until the rattle in her chest died away and her head rested peacefully on the palm of my hand. When I finally carried her back to the box I was not sure she was alive. I did not expect her to live. But she did, for another six years.

During convalescence she became very exacting, in a charming way. Before she would consent to retire for the night, certain ceremonies had to be performed. The first was the Butterfly Game.

To amuse her I had made what looked something like a butterfly out of cellophane attached to a long, thin wire. This I had to make fly through the air, as realistically as possible. If it did not look enough like a butterfly she grunted and turned her head, then resorted to coughing to let me know she was displeased.

At first she could do no more than watch the butterfly, following its course with eager eyes as it flitted about, to light on the wall, on the box, sometimes, sending a delighted shudder down her back, right on one of her paws. But as she gained strength she pursued with more and more zest, until the Butterfly Game turned into a most energetic romp.

When she grew tired she went willingly to bed, but not to sleep. Next came the washing ceremony, in which she did all the work. Very thoroughly she washed my hand, the back of it, the palm, the fingers, the wrist, occasionally getting in a few licks on her own fur. And after that I was required to hold her paw until she fell asleep, which fortunately didn't take long. But let me withdraw a moment too soon and she was wide awake again, demanding that everything start over, beginning with the Butterfly Game.

At first she would not eat voluntarily unless I held the

plate, but in time she made a concession. It would be all right if I put just one finger on the plate. But let me withdraw the finger for only an instant, say to scratch my nose, and the deal was off. She would not continue eating until I had apologized and promised never to do such a thing again.

She was fussy. If one crumb fell off the plate it had to be cleaned up before she would go on eating. Moreover, the food had to be consumed according to a pattern, which varied according to her mood. Sometimes she ate exactly half of what was on the plate, the line across the center cut as sharp as if by a knife, the clean side thoroughly polished. Other times she would cut out a wedge, like a piece of a pie. Or she would go all around the edges, leaving a precise mound in the middle.

Even when she was totally well she retained some of the peculiarities acquired during her illness. She had got used to sleeping with a blanket over her and still wanted it there, no matter how warm the night. Even during the day she would nudge at the blanket, indicating she wished to be covered, and I would drape it over her head and shoulders, fastening it under chin with a safety pin, to leave her sitting contentedly purring, looking like a little old Russian grandmamma dozing before the firelight.

When I went away for an evening she would try to cover herself. I would come home to find the rug honey-combed with tunnels, a little mound at the end of one. Then another game had to be played. I had to pretend I couldn't find her, call and search and wonder where she was, until at last my hands came upon the little mound.

"There she is!" I would exclaim, and she would crawl out from the tunnel to greet me with a cry of delight.

She never begged, for either food or affection. I suppose that was why it was so easy for me to forget. As our family of cats grew I had less and less time to give her the attention she'd gotten used to. I mislaid her butterfly, forgot about the game. If she left her dinner untouched, I did not hold the plate, only took it away and offered it again later.

Nor did I give her medicine for another illness invading her body. There was nothing I could give, but how was she to know that? How was she to know that while I was busy taking care of others I worried about her?

On the last day, Kate was bitten by a snake, and I had to work hard to save her life. All my attention was given to her, as once it had been given to Moire. Moire waited a while longer, then chose not to wait.

For some time she sat at the side of the road, watching the cars go by. Neighbors remarked on it and told me later. Perhaps she was waiting for me to call? Waiting for me to find her and exclaim, "Why, there she is!"

She let the cars go by, one after the other, then stepped in front of one. Some little boys came to tell me. They had seen it happen.

I put down a blanket and folded it around her for the last time, and carried her home.

The Mother Cat

The runt of a litter, Cricket was so stunted that even in maturity she still looked like just a half grown kitten. Moreover, she had a handicap. Being a Manx, she had no tail to erect when she was pleased, to lash when she was angry, to seductively writhe like a snake for the enjoyment of possible offspring. Nevertheless, she was the matriarch of the family, the all-embracing Mother, always ready to defend, console or administer aid to all the other cats. If, for instance, I inadvertently stepped on someone's tail, thus provoking a surprised hiss or growl, I had to apologize not only to the injured party but even more fervently to her.

I was also expected to grant her little favors, like being allowed to nurse her kitten on my bed. I say kitten, in the singular, because, favoring quality over quantity, she seldom produced more than one. So when the man knocked on the door and handed me what looked like a wet bedraggled piece of fur, Cricket was on the bed with her current kitten, an amiable fellow named Chowder because he was a little bit of everything, including the Manx inherited from his mother, with, therefore, only a stub of a tail to wiggle.

The piece of fur the man had brought turned out to be a tiny orphaned raccoon, very unhappy and very hungry. After I had dried her off and fed her bread and milk from the palm of my hand, a messy procedure, I found myself literally attached to her. Her paws were like burrs that fastened tight on any part of me they encountered. So I named her Thistle, and with considerable difficulty managed to transfer her to a warm nest of blankets, where she promptly started shrieking that she was being totally murdered.

She was, of course, lonely. Would cats make suitable companions? They were the same size, more or less, mostly considerably more, I had to admit. Nevertheless, a tentative introduction was made, and was followed by an immediate mass exodus of the cats. With one accord they took refuge on high shelves, as far as possible from the stranger's obnoxious smell. All, that is, except Cricket. She remained stolidly hunched on the bed, allowing Chowder to continue chewing on one of her ears. Her nostrils were just as offended by the smell, but maternal instincts prevailed. What was presented to her was an utterly miserable creature sorely in need of mothering.

Grunting an invitation, she rolled over on her side to offer her milk. Eagerly the raccoon nudged against the proffered belly, searched and nuzzled. But something was wrong. Mouth and nipple just didn't seem to fit. But at least Cricket became half a mother, administering, comforting and protecting. I, provider of food, was the other half.

Emulating the other cats, Chowder at once had stopped demolishing his mother's ear and backed away from the unpleasant odor. Then the proverbial curiosity of the cat got the better of him, and warily he crept toward the strange creature who had usurped his place near his mother, and upon cautious inspection made a fascinating discovery. It had a tail, a fine, furry, busy tail that twitched when he tapped it and squirmed delightfully under a capturing paw.

Abandoning her quest for milk, Thistle protested, but youth is goodnatured, and what threatened to become a battle turned into a game, the two of them rolling about locked together, parting to flee and pursue, leap and pounce and engage in a boxing match, with Mother Cricket watching approvingly. And that night at bedtime she had two youngsters snuggled up against her, one of which she washed for a long time, to make it smell more like a cat.

Her efforts were so successful that even Thistle herself believed she was a cat. At least she behaved like one. True, her socializing with the older cats consisted mainly of teasing them if she thought she could get away with it, but her relationship to Chowder was one of sibling affection. By the hour they played, chasing each other from room to room and back again, up onto chairs and down, in and out of cardboard boxes until, in sudden accord, they fell asleep in one of the boxes, with an approving Cricket frequently joining them.

But with the incipient maturity came variances. Engaged in a heedless caper one day, Chowder accidentally pushed open the little swinging door that provided feline egress to the outside world. Gazing with awe at the immensity that lay beyond, he made a tentative exit and scrambled back in again, tried to repeat the maneuver, lost his footing and tumbled down the steps. Of course Thistle tumbled after him, to stand petrified by her boldness until Chowder distracted her by pursuing a leaf. She joined him, and this turned into a fine game of tag until Chowder veered off to climb a tree.

It must be that infant raccoons have to be taught to climb, as it is said ducklings are taught to swim. While Chowder cavorted among the branches, Thistle laboriously hauled her bulkier body up the trunk of the tree, only to have Chowder skip lightly over and past her to scramble down again, leaving her precariously slumped in a crotch, shrieking in terror. Of course, Mother Cricket had to come to the rescue.

Cricket was afraid of trees. Never had she climbed one more than a couple of feet, to make a trembling descent as if scaling down a mountain. But she was a mother. When an offspring is in danger, a mother is fearless.

With a fine show of bravery she climbed all the way to the crotch where Thistle was cowering, then with little reassuring grunts showed her how to come down, but in such terror of her own that she could hardly transfer her weight from one shaking paw to the other. Thistle followed head first, like a proper raccoon, wrapping her stubby back legs around the trunk of the tree and digging the claws in like crampons. This method of traveling turned out to be so agreeable that, once down, she had to prove climbing a tree was no big deal by clambering right back up again, to Cricket's utter dismay.

It was Chowder, the intrepid explorer, who found the pool in back of the house. Both he and Thistle were already acquainted with water. Thistle loved to find the tap in the bathtub turned on so she could put one of her dexterous paws over the nozzle and spray a stream of water that almost always caught Chowder off guard and sent him fleeing. But such a large body of water as the pool demanded respect. Chowder prowled cautiously along the

bank. Thistle went into a typical raccoon shuffle of indecision, approaching and retreating, until she found the
courage to dip one paw into the water, then fled to hide
behind Cricket.

But unlike cats, raccoons are at home in water. Lured
back to the pool, Thistle ceased to be a cat. Again she
dipped in her paws, then with little sniffles of indecision
slid her whole body into this strange but enticing element,
went wading to a depth that changed the wading to
paddling, and so learned how to swim. Meanwhile Chowder took himself elsewhere, and Cricket, her mothering
divided, went the more practical way to watch over
Chowder.

Other differences became evident. Chowder didn't
like visitors. Whenever they arrived, he departed. Thistle
adored visitors, greeted them with an enthusiasm that
seldom was reciprocated. Most people didn't enjoy having their legs climbed, their fingers chewed, their watches
removed, their ears, nostrils and hair explored. Only
youngsters, yipping and yelping, giggling and groaning,
had a perfectly wonderful time submitting to Thistle's
mauling.

But entranced though she might be by such diver-
sions, Thistle still remained loyal to her foster mother and
brother. At the end of each day of strenuous activity the
three of them were always bedded together, Thistle having
reached such proportions that folds of her flesh overflowed to almost entirely conceal the diminutive Cricket
and slender Chowder.

Then the time came when, inseparable as they were,

they had to be separated. Soon after his birth Chowder had been promised to a friend, and now he was old enough to go to his new home, halfway across the continent. One moment he was still with Thistle as usual. The next moment he was gone. Just gone.

She couldn't believe in his absence, refused to believe. All through the house she searched, peering behind doors and under furniture and in corners, trilling to him invitingly. Outside she looked in all the places he favored, climbed tree after tree in the hope of finding him hiding among the branches.

When she finally gave up, it was completely, entirely, totally. Slumped in a corner she presented a picture of utter despair, head bowed, usually busy hands lying on her belly like a tired old peasant woman's. Nothing could engage her interest.

It was time for her to go, too. So one dark quiet night I opened the door and invited her to go out with me. On this and following nights she found nothing much to her liking and came back indoors immediately. Then she discovered that if she climbed a tree and walked along one of its branches, she could reach the roof. Looking down on the world from this height seemed to please her, and she spent more and more time up there.

It seemed no harm could come to her in such a protected location, but after I had gone indoors one night I heard an odd thumping overhead, and sounds of squabbling, like children arguing over something, occasionally punctuated by somewhat ominous yelps. Of course as foster mother I had to run to the rescue, and was at once immobilized by a most awesome sight. At the sound of my approach a veritable cascade of raccoons, what looked like a torrent of raccoons, spilled over the edge of the roof, thudded to the ground and scampered away. There was no sign of Thistle.

Four days passed with no sign of her and I had to conclude that she had met with disaster when her sanctuary on the roof had been invaded. But just before dawn of the fifth day I was awakened by a persistent pounding on the door. When I opened it there was Thistle, apparently first in command of a whole gang of raccoons, all demanding admittance. Somehow she must have conveyed to them the information that I was good for a handout.

So I was. While they invaded the house, sending the cats, even Cricket, leaping to the safety of high shelves, I hastily broke open a box of cookies and enticed the invaders, one by one, out into the night. Graciously accepting her cookie, Thistle went with them.

Thus the raccoon who had believed she was a cat finally became an accredited member of a family living in the woods, and Cricket, who had been half her mother, went back to being a proper cat, every now and then producing a kitten with no tail.

The Wild Cat

I felt him before I saw him. That's how it is sometimes: I stand in the night and know I am not alone. My
surveillant may be only a deer mouse, staring down with
fascination and uncertainty from the branch of a hemlock
tree, or a screech owl, head cocked at a ludicrous angle, as
if pasted on wrong. This time, the beam of my flashlight
played around me reflected a pair of round eyes.

He was some distance away, a shimmering phantom
that looked like a cat but was too large to be one, and as he
turned I saw that he had no tail. Then he was gone. I
thought perhaps I had seen a bobcat.

The next night, again I felt myself being watched.
The stars were bright in a clear sky and when my eyes had
adjusted to their light I saw him, a dim shadow pacing
warily around me. I switched on the flashlight, caught the
gleam of eyes and the shimmer of light fur. Then where he
had been there was nothing.

The following evening I put down a plate of cat food
near the tree. He did not take it. The next night I tried raw

meat. He waited until I went indoors, then came back and ate.

For many nights after that I sat on the steps, not moving even when the mosquitoes found and feasted on me, waiting for the shadow to come out of the deeper shadow of the woods. He would warily approach the plate of meat, stare hard at the place where I sat, and finally I'd hear his lips smacking as he ate.

Gradually the time of waiting shortened, until he came as soon as I had settled on the steps. I moved then, each night a little closer to the dish, until I could put my hand on it, palm up. After he had gotten used to that I took away the plate and put the meat on the palm of my hand. When he nosed over the fingers, the palm, the wrist, his whiskers sent almost painful chills up my arm, but he ate with great care, as if aware of my vulnerability.

Then I dared touch him. As soon as he had taken the last bite of meat, while he was still chewing, I turned the hand over to touch the top of his head. He ducked and ran the first time, and the second time, but finally accepted the caress, then allowed the hand to stroke him, going gradually down his back until I could slip it under his belly.

Each night I lifted him a little more and a little more, until finally I dared pick him up, and on my lap he purred. We had become friends.

We had grown acquainted in the dark, with only the light of the stars to see by. Now that I had his trust I carried him over to the window for a better look. He was honey-colored, with slightly darker stripes that shaded to lavender on the top of his head. He was larger than a house cat, with broad, powerful shoulders, but he was not a bobcat. He was a Manx.

Where this breed originated no one really knows. It is said that such tailless cats were aboard the Spanish Armada, and when one of the ships was wrecked near the Isle of Man a pair swam ashore, where they survived and multiplied. The one certainty is that, however he came there, the Manx cat is now native to the Isle of Man.

In the early eighteen-hundreds, some sailors, sons of a New Jersey farmer, brought a few of the Manx to this country, where their offspring eventually "went wild."

Bobs

Now, about a hundred and fifty years later, there is still a scattering of such wild Manx in the woods of New Jersey and New York, but they are growing scarce. Bobs must have been one of these.

Where he spent his days I did not know, but after we had become friends he posted himself each night on the back steps, to guard them until dawn. Whenever I opened the door he would at once stand at attention, and wherever I went out of doors he followed—until I entered a building. He would not go with me into the barn, or the hay shed, or the house, all of which he must have thought were huge traps. As long as the weather was good his keeping such a vigil on the steps didn't bother me. But I couldn't stand seeing him squatting there in the pelting rain. And what about the snows to come?

In the hope that he had grown to trust me enough, I hollowed out a bed for him in the hay barn. He was now quite used to being carried. Surely he would trust me enough to let me carry him into the shed? In a cold miserable drizzle he walked with me as far as the door. I went in, put down a blanket, then came out and picked him up. He purred as always until we were through the doorway. Then he made no sound at all but suddenly gripped my head between his forelegs, and dug his claws into my scalp. Had I cried out I'm sure he would have mangled me, but I also made no sound, only turned and walked out again. Back in the rain he withdrew his claws, let go of my head and in a moment was purring again. Quite simply, his devotion to me was not strong enough to overcome his fear of traps.

Then it occurred to me I could make him a doghouse. First I put down a platform, with a blanket on it. He liked that. I gave the platform one side, after an interval another side, then a third, and a fourth with an entrance hole cut in it. He learned to go through the hole, and enjoyed lying on the blanket. Then came the crucial top, removable, in case he objected to it. But he had watched the house being built, had grown accustomed to entering the doorway. He lay down on the blanket and purred.

Was it warm enough? I put in my hand to stroke him, felt the vibration of his purring but also a draft. This brought out the sewing machine, to make a pair of curtains for the doorway. I think those curtains entranced Bobs as much as they did me. I never tired of watching him nudge against the folds to locate the opening, and taking pride in the way they fell shut after his round rump had passed through.

Toward my other resident cats he was gravely amiable, but no strange cat, or dog of any size, was allowed to set foot upon our land. Even some humans, it seemed, did so at their peril.

One day I glanced out of the window and caught sight of a man, a neighbor I did not particularly like, standing rigidly still on our path, about halfway to the house. Around him Bobs was stalking a menacing circle, gradually closing in, in appearance so wild that I shared the man's concern. I hurried out.

"Call him off," the man said, hardly moving his lips. "He's about to spring."

"Bobs," I said, without raising my voice. At once a

tame cat came to me, turning only once to give the man a last long look of hatred. In my arms he purred, and we watched the man lope off, having changed his mind about paying a visit.

Later this man was caught poisoning cats. Was Bobs aware of this evil? Did he smell it on the man, or had he merely sensed and duplicated my own dislike? I didn't know, but at least the man never came back. Perhaps, facing Bobs, he came to smell his own evil.

Along with keeping off trespassers, Bobs had other duties. Twice a day, in the morning and the evening, he helped me with the chores. Whenever the weather was favorable some of the other cats might follow me, but Bobs did not follow. He led. When fresh snow lay on the ground he broke trail for me, not I for him. From rabbit cage to the hay shed to the barn to the water hole—he knew the way better than I. With thoughts on other matters, too often I had to retrace my steps, either because I had forgotten something or couldn't remember whether I had forgotten or not. Bobs eliminated such uncertainty. As long as I did each chore properly he trotted ahead, glancing over his shoulder now and then to make sure I was coming along. But if I deviated from routine anywhere along the way he barred my path. At first I did not understand and simply stepped over him. Swiftly he would circle around to stop me again. Once I came to understand I'd say, "What have I forgotten? Oh, yes!" and Bobs, knowing I was on the right track, would come as close to dancing as dignity allowed.

Like the proverbial postman, he was deterred from

making appointed rounds by neither rain nor snow, nor wind. During a violent storm that drove rain straight across instead of down, I begged him to stay home. He would not. After only half the chores were done I took him back and put him in his house, but at once he was out, looking irked, to lead the way through the rain to where we had left off.

Only on rare occasions did he desert me, and then gave fair warning. Whenever he ate the half pound of meat that was his daily ration and asked for more, I knew that we were going to have a snowstorm and he was leaving.

He never went away before the light falls, but only when we were to get several feet or more. Somewhere he must have had a cave or a burrow that had once been his home, and some wild instinct left in him told him he should hole up there. Always, as soon as the storm was over, he would be back, breaking trail for me. Why snow made him depart and never rain was a question only he could answer.

Except for such brief defections, he was for three years a partner so unfailing that I finally took him for granted. But in the fall of the third year, when he was in his prime, a big fellow with powerful muscles and a thick, gleaming coat, I somehow became aware of the fact that he was, like all of us, mortal. He showed no sign of illness. His eyes were bright and clear. His appetite was excellent. Yet after he had finished eating I would take him on my lap to examine him closely, filled with a strange persistent foreboding. I tried to memorize his beauty, stroked him often so I should not forget the vibrant feel of him under my hand, tricked him into posing for a few pictures. He feared the camera as if it was a lethal weapon, but I hid it under my coat, snapped hastily and hid it again. The pictures didn't turn out well. My farewell pictures never do.

As the days grew shorter I spent more and more time with him, making sure he did not go out on the road or too far into the woods, knowing this would only make the hurt that much greater when he left. Shortly before the hunting season I built a cage, entirely of wire so that he would not feel confined, and put his house in it, with the blanket that was familiar to him. Because he had watched the cage being built he had no fear of it, and when the season opened stayed there each day, curled up on his blanket, until the hunters left at sundown. Then he did the evening chores with me and enjoyed freedom until just before I went to bed, when I fed him and put him back in the cage.

I found it difficult to make the morning chores without him. Everything went topsy-turvy, and I could not shake off a feeling of sadness and loss, as if he'd already gone. But in the evening we made up for the drabness of the day. He had never before indulged in play. Now his customary gravity was flung to the wind that chased dry leaves across our path. Having made sure I was headed in the right direction, he would go off on a tangent to cut a caper, pursue a phantom up the trunk of a tree or roll over with a captured stone hugged to his belly, back legs kicking it into pretend resistance. Yet no matter how preoccupied he seemed to be, the game was instantly abandoned when one chore was done and it was time to lead me to another.

I never knew what he did after I went indoors, and had misgivings that he might not return to be put back in his cage. But night after night when I called there would at once be a rustling in the dry leaves, and I would see his light coat shimmering as he came out from the dark woods. I held him on my lap while I fed him, and for as long afterward as I could bear the cold. Then side by side we walked to the cage, he hopped in, and I closed the door.

I counted down the days of the hunting season, from fifteen to five ... four ... three ... two, and with each one ticked off my uneasiness lessened. My hunch had been wrong. Bobs would not leave.

The next to the last day of the season was cold and gloomy. While we did the evening chores a few flakes of snow fell, just a few. I parted from Bobs, watched him trot off into the woods without misgivings. During the evening I did not worry about him, and, preoccupied with something I was working on, I even neglected to go out, as was my custom to check on the weather. So I was totally unprepared for, could not believe what I saw when at bedtime I opened the door to go out and call Bobs.

It must have snowed all evening. Over two feet lay on the ground and the air was heavy, almost solid, with more coming down, silently, steadily. This was a big storm, the kind that always made Bobs hole up. If I had fed him earlier, as was the custom before the hunting season, he would have given me warning, asking for double rations. Now it was too late. The expanse of white lay unbroken all around. Nowhere could I see any tracks or depressions where tracks might have been made earlier. I called, and the sound of my voice pressed close around me, muffled by the snow, as if I were shouting inside thick walls. I waded through the snow to the cage. He was not there. I went to the road, calling. The lamps glittered behind the white curtain, casting down wavering pools of light. No small shadow came plodding out of the dark to shimmer under them.

I blamed myself for not having fed and caged him earlier, for ignoring the east wind's warning and those first few flakes of snow, for neglecting to go out all evening, for relaxing vigilance just now, almost at the end. Twice more I went out and called, then sat in the snow for a while, trying to feel close to him, wherever he was. "Stay there," I begged. "You must be very hungry, but stay there. Don't try to come back until it is dark again."

The next day the sun shone, the snow sparkled, a fine day, made for gaiety. Far away children were shouting and laughing, and farther still, shots split the brittle air. I saw bird and squirrel tracks all about the house, but none made by a cat.

For a week I did the morning chores in a vast loneliness, and waited for him in the evening, with fear in the pit of my stomach, to finally make the rounds by flashlight, in the dark. And each night I went out to sit near his house, not calling, just waiting.

Then I heard what had happened. On that fine morning when the sun shone, the birds and squirrels sported over the snow, children played and laughed, a boy from the village, wandering through the woods, had come upon some tracks, six in all, five made by heavy hunters' boots, the sixth by a deer, and alongside the last were bright red drops of blood. The boy recognized the imprints as those of a doe, and knew following would be dangerous. In such evil days his life would be considered of less value than the fine the hunters would have to pay if caught with a doe. But, curious and perhaps indignant, he walked the way the tracks went, through the snow, up a hill, across a meadow, over a stone wall, into dense woods beyond. There, near a thicket, he found the doe, her body still warm.

Tracks showed the five hunters had gathered around her, then scattered, each pair of boots going in a different direction. A shot rang out, not far away. The boy went toward the sound, through the woods, to the stone wall, and that was how he came upon Bobs, on the other side of the wall.

He must have made a fine target, leaping over the wall, and I suppose hitting it made the hunter feel better about having to give up the doe. What was one cat more or less in a world where human life was cheap? What matter that this one had had an appointment to keep?

Once more the chores went askew and I had to retrace steps, to do what I had forgotten or to make sure I had not forgotten. Yet I remembered too well how he looked trotting solemnly ahead of me, how his vibrant body felt under my hand, how he lay trusting on my lap to gaze up at me. I didn't need pictures.

But so much has been forgotten. Will he some day be forgotten, too?

That is the worst of bereavement, the forgetting, the image growing a little fainter each time one tries to find comfort in its evocation, until at last it is gone entirely, as dead as the death that took it away.

There Was A Cat

I was acquainted with him long before I knew him. Every once in a while I would see him, a big tiger cat with white markings on chest and feet, nosing around the area where I fed the birds, squirrels, chipmunks and whatever else came that way for a handout. Usually by the time he arrived most of the food would be gone, but occasionally he would come upon a piece of suet fallen from the feeder, a great prize that he seized and carried off to consume somewhere in the woods. Undoubtedly he was homeless, and having a hard time making it on his own.

I tried to favor him, hurrying out to offer a handful of whatever was handy, but he didn't even wait for me to appear. As soon as he heard the door open he was off, bounding away in panic. I tried calling, "Kitty, Kitty?" thinking that word might evoke memory of a pleasant relationship, but that only hastened his departure. On the off chance that he would return I left food for him and stayed out of sight. The food remained untouched until someone else came along to claim it.

Bad treatment must have taught him to mistrust all humans, even one who welcomed him and pleaded with him to accept the sustenance he needed.

As I said, I was acquainted with him for some time. Year after year I caught glimpses of him through the window, in summer hovering on the outskirts of a group of feasting raccoons, in winter darting in among long-legged wild turkeys to pick up what morsels he could.

Even with no encouragement from me the raccoons had become tame. So had the wild turkeys. The cat must have noticed that they trusted me. Yet he remained wild.

His appearances were far from regular. I would see him one day in the morning, another in the evening. Sometimes weeks would pass with no sign of him, and I'd say, "Poor fellow, I suppose that's the last of him," and then he would turn up again, as fearful as ever.

In the spring of the year there is a short hiatus in which the turkeys withdraw to the woods to breed and raise their young, and raccoons are preoccupied with augmenting their species. In one such lull, in perhaps the sixth or seventh year of the cat's appearances, I discovered that the birds and squirrels, faithful dependents the year round, had grown fond of cat chow. So I stocked up on sacks of chow and put out generous feedings.

The cat had no reason to fear the squirrels and birds, nor it turned out, had they any reason to fear him. Almost every morning I was witness to the same scene, the cat hurriedly crunching down cat pellets, the birds and squirrels darting about him to pick up their share.

Then one morning as I put out the food I heard a cry

at the edge of the woods, some distance away. There was no mistaking the sound. The cat was speaking to me. I answered. He spoke again. And so it was from then on, with his venturing each day a little closer, a little closer, only to suddenly take fright and dart back into the woods.

When it finally came at last, his surrender was abrupt and complete. When I went outside one day he was there at my feet, talking volubly. Startled, I said, "Well, how you do jabber!" which was in error, of course. What he said in his language probably made sense, may even have been profound. But anyway, that was how he got his name. I called him Jabber.

He answered readily, but I seldom had to call him. Now whenever I was out of doors he was at my side, just there, not asking for attention, making no demands, only responding eagerly to the touch of my hand. When I was indoors he sat on the steps, ready to stand at attention if the door opened, or on the shelf outside the kitchen window—with some discomfort, surely, because the shelf was really too narrow to accommodate his bulk—watching as I moved about inside, complacently ignoring the insults my house cat hurled at him. If the house cat had not been so hostile I might have invited him in and perhaps things would have turned out differently. But perhaps not. Fate can be very stubborn.

Even when he went for a stroll on his own—he was meticulous about traveling some distance from the house for sanitary purposes—he kept close watch and joined me as soon as I appeared outside. Wherever I walked, he walked with me. If I sat to rest for a while on a log or a boulder he settled at once at my feet, to gaze around with satisfaction at a world that by some miracle had become friendly to him. He had a home. He had someone to love. His eyes shone with happiness.

When he stopped talking to me as usual I thought little of it. He feels secure now, I reasoned. He no longer feels he has to keep assuring me of his devotion. When after we had rested for a while in the woods and he did not return home with me but stayed where he had settled in the leaves at my feet, I told myself that was good. Like all the others, he was beginning to take me for granted, no longer had to fear he would lose me.

But when he was not immediately in attendance one morning I had sudden misgivings. He should at least be eager for his breakfast. I called, saw movement at the edge of the woods, and watched as he came to me as fast as he could walk, shuffling like an old, old man.

How old was he?

At my feet he gazed at me and at the food I offered, then turned and sat down with his back to me, and I understood what he was telling me. He was ill.

For some moments he stayed with his back to me like that, not moving. Then he got to his feet and walked slowly away, back to vanish in the woods, and I understood that, too. He had come to me one last time to say goodbye.

I wish fate had been kinder, had let him go gently on a nest of dry leaves under a benign sun. But rain started falling, fell relentlessly for two days. I searched knowing I could not find him. Somewhere, in some rain-soaked sanctuary, he departed as he had lived, without comfort, alone.

I was glad I had been allowed to give him that brief time of the happiness he deserved, and bitter because it was so brief. But there is nowhere to direct the bitterness, except toward those humans out there somewhere who sentenced him to all those terrible years of deprivation, loneliness and fear.

Era Zistel

Bunky

A Cat by Another Name

His owner died and he was destined to be "put down," as the British say, so I agreed to take him in.

He was six years old, without doubt the dullest, most stupid, indifferent cat I'd ever met. For a while I thought he might be deaf. Indeed, if I clapped my hands behind his back there was no response. But he heard well enough when the refrigerator door or a can was opened.

I was told his name was Tommy, which he failed to acknowledge with even the slightest flick of an ear, and I couldn't say I blamed him. I tried other names close enough in sound so that he wouldn't be confused, if that were possible, but Johnny, Sonny, Donny and various other admittedly unimaginative appellations were also ignored.

In truth I didn't get much chance to call him anything at all because I saw very little of him. After discovering the upper bunk, then not in use for other purposes, he spent most of his time up there, climbing down only to eat and use the litter box meticulously and ardently, with much fierce scratching.

I matched his indifference with my own until one day, when he descended from the bunk for one of his two functions, I took notice of him with a greeting of "Hi, Bunky!" expecting no response as usual, but the words had a startling effect.

As if I'd touched a button to activate him, suddenly he came alive. Lifting his head to look at me with eyes that were all at once bright and friendly, he answered me with a cheerful grunt.

From then on he was a different cat. Of course, I couldn't say that calling him Bunky had brought about the change. Perhaps my doing so just happened to coincide with his recovery from grief over the loss of someone he had loved. Or perhaps he'd never been given much attention, and had at last been drawn out of defensive aloofness by my persistent friendliness.

Whatever the reason for the onset of this new relationship, it led to my discovering that he was anything but stupid. Eagerly responding to whatever I said, he soon acquired a rudimentary knowledge of my language.

The one word I consider essential for the maintenance of good relations between humans and animals is the word "no." To elicit the proper response from Bunky I didn't have to shout or even raise my voice above conversational level. Whenever he heard me say no, whatever he happened to be doing came to an abrupt halt. Even when merely walking across the room, he immediately reversed direction.

Now that we were friends his one desire, it seemed, was to please me, no matter how inconvenient or difficult that might be. My asking him to "get out," for instance, was a nuisance, requesting as it did that he vacate whatever location he happened to be in. His alacrity in obeying both amused and pleased me, and proved most convenient when he really was in the way.

In fact, so prompt was he in carrying out my wishes that I began to wonder, with a touch of unease, how much of what I spoke he understood beyond the words he had learned. And my thoughts? Did he know them, too?

He had come to me at a time when my interest in wildlife had grown paramount and I had arrived at the decision that, since cats are predators, any I harbored would have to be kept strictly indoors. Now there was the problem of what to do about Bunky. It seemed unfair to deny him a pleasure he had taken for granted in his previous life. But I couldn't allow indiscriminate slaughtering of the small animals that had come to trust me.

Could there be a compromise? Could Bunky be given freedom out of doors for a short time each day, under strict supervision? We might try it, I thought, and if he proved unmanageable I'd simply have to keep him indoors.

As if he knew precisely what those terms were he remained close by my side on our walks, with only short excursions a few feet this way or that, to read some story the earth had to tell him. On rainy days we stayed in the barn, I performing some chore or other while he watched me work, or sat in the doorway with his thoughts and his paws turned inward, gazing through half closed eyes at the curtain of rain outside.

Of course the inevitable happened. Not far from us

one day a chipmunk chattered a challenge and, obeying instinct, Bunky lunged to capture it. Automatically I shouted, "No!" and to my disbelief Bunky almost skidded to a stop. "Good Bunky, good Bunky," I murmured, and responding to the praise he sinuated his body against my leg.

Having learned that for some inexplicable reason I wished chipmunks to be left unmolested, he resolutely ignored their trillings from then on, no matter how they taunted him. But birds were a different problem. It was unreasonable to expect any cat to refrain from reacting in a perfectly normal way to all the chirpings and flutterings of such temptingly delicate creatures. And, unusual though Bunky might be in many respects, he was after all a normal cat. Was it at all possible to persuade him to be not normal?

The birds were fed in an area of the yard just in front of the house. Could this area be declared out of bounds for Bunky? I avoided going there myself when he was with me, but sometimes even then he gravitated in that direction. A "no" always brought him back, looking frustrated and bewildered. But the temptation the birds offered was too great, as was the strain on me of constantly maintaining watch.

Was there a way to keep him out of the area entirely? I thought of how effective the words "get out" had been, and decided to give that a try. Instead of constantly saying "no" I took up a stand in the area where the birds were feeding and shouted, "Get out!" Bunky comprehended almost immediately. Unreasonable though it was, the area where the birds were had been declared forbidden territory.

This lesson was learned so well that visitors were sometimes confounded. Arriving at the front door they would see him in back and call to him, "Hi, Bunky!" Always he would run toward them eagerly, then come to a halt at an invisible boundary line.

"What's the matter?" the visitors would ask. "Why won't he come to us?" And I'd have to give the implausible explanation, "Because he's not allowed."

In exchange for his obedience to my rules, he demanded respect for some of his own. His dinner had to be served in a location of his choosing, precisely, if you please, not varying an inch one way or the other. When dinner time came he would go to this place, make a smart turnabout like a soldier to indicate the exact location, then sit down to give me a look, firm but polite, that said, "Right here, please."

The same militant precision was evident outside. When I had work to do in the barn and the day was fair, he would take up a stand just before the door on a patch of ground where soon a circle of grass the exact size of his rump was worn away. Having made the turn like a good soldier, he would remain seated there as immobile as a soldier on guard, only turning his head ever so slightly to check on some sound or movement in the vicinity, until I said, "Let's go home," and he was instantly off to lead the way.

His devotion was almost an embarrassment. Yet his demands were modest. He never begged for affection or even attention. He was not a lap cat, for which I was grateful. He was such a big fellow that his weight would have been a burden. Instead he placed himself wherever I sat down, with his usual precision, always in the same spot, in front of my left foot. It is said a cat will not look you in the eye for long. His gaze was so unwavering that always my eyes were the first to turn away.

With the passage of time his attachment seemed to become almost an obsession. No matter where I went, even if only to cross the room, he was close beside my feet. And whenever I was still somewhere, anywhere, he would fix upon me that long steady gaze of such depth that it actually made me uneasy. It was almost as if he feared that if he lost sight of me I might vanish.

Could he have sensed what was coming? Could he have *known*?

I was suddenly taken ill and hospitalized for six months. We didn't even have a chance to say goodbye.

The Problem Cat

When the boys brought him to me, asking, "Will you give this one a home?" knowing full well the answer would be affirmative, he was just a kitten, too young to have been taken away from his mother. But even at that tender age he was quite handsome, wearing a thick maltese coat trimmed with white bib and boots, gazing at me with large, extraordinarily beautiful opal eyes.

During the first days of his residence he seemed normal enough, although he did not cry for his mother like most infants and showed no distress at being set down in a totally strange environment. With the utmost complacency he accepted a new home and a new human to cater to his needs.

Then, once he had acquainted himself with those aspects of his surroundings he considered worthy of his interest, and memorized two important locations, where food was dispensed and it was proper to eliminate, he acquired a distinct personality, shockingly evil.

Spurning my receptive lap and all overtures toward friendship, he purred only when contemplating something close to mayhem. Hands reaching down to stroke him were met with slashing talons. Picking him up turned out to be impossible. Instantly flipping over on his back he would gyrate wildly, bristling with razor sharp teeth and needle-like claws. Yet in this display there was never any evidence of malice. The friendly hand was slashed with the utmost geniality, as if a favor were being conferred. He even purred.

Puzzling over this unusual behavior, I wondered whether I had made a mistake in naming him Rrou after a book by that title, remembering too late that the cat in the book had been fiercely independent. Perhaps in conferring that name on an impressionable kitten I had imbued him with a matching personality?

Then I read a book about malfunctions of the brain and learned that disorders of the hypothalamus at the base of the brain, triggered odd behavior in both humans and animals, one manifestation of which is an uncontrollable urge to bite. Could Rrou have been brain damaged at birth?

Whatever the reason for his propensity to inflict pain, one thing was certain: he was my cat, irrevocably, because nobody else would have him. Nursing my wounds, generously distributed over all of me but my face, for which he seemed to have great respect, I tried to find a way to not only live with him but make him acceptable to others.

Unfortunately, he loved people, or at any rate most people. Whenever anyone came to the door he raced with me to get there first, so he could greet visitors with a most disarming show of friendliness until a hand reached down to pet him. Invariably the hand was bitten.

"I'm sorry," I'd apologize. "He really likes you. He just has a peculiar way of showing it."

For most visitors this was hardly reassuring, especially if Rrou remained in attendance to launch further attacks on their feet. Sometimes, though, he would lose interest and wander off, but wherever he went he never failed to detect preparatory sounds of departure, and would come hurrying back to function as a perfect host by escorting guests to the door, bidding them farewell with a great leap to inflict a final laceration.

Before long people either stayed away entirely or took the precaution of inquiring through the closed door, "Can you get rid of Rrou?" This in turn was hard on me, because persuading him to dispense with his welcoming duties always led to some shedding of my own blood.

All these assaults on people were made without rancor except on two occasions. A woman who was really fond of cats and tried hard to make friends with him was so fiercely set upon that she was quite badly wounded. The fact that I myself didn't particularly care for the woman seemed insufficient justification for the violence of the attack, but I could think of no other.

The second victim was an electrician who came to give an estimate on replacing some wiring. Rrou took one sniff at him and gave him a truly vicious bite in the ankle. For this I admit I may have been to blame, for my own aversion to the man was such that, even though distressed, I found myself murmuring under my breath, "Good for you, Rrou!" Needless to say, the electrician decided he couldn't do the job. Needless to say, I did not try to change his mind.

So there I was, sharing my house with a strange creature I did not dare touch, even had to avoid most of the time. Friends asked, "How can you stand him?" and sometimes, examining my scarred hands, arms and legs, I asked myself the same question.

But—

In the first place, he was a challenge. Was there any possibility of altering his obnoxious behavior? Then, too, he was so persistently good-natured, so cheerful, so eager to please in his own macabre way that, even while nursing a slashed finger I found him somewhat endearing. With his big round eyes shining with such deceptive innocence

Photo by Richard Winter

Rrou

he could be most charming. And he was disarmingly devoted.

Wherever I went I had his company, even in the bathtub, where he never failed to crouch on the rim to supervise my bathing. Most cats are afraid of water. Not Rrou. Its mysterious liquidity fascinated him. Dipping in his paws, he would scoop it up to give me a good splashing. If I retaliated by flinging water over him he responded with glee, splashing even harder, with such fervor that he would almost lose his balance and fall in. Only when he was thoroughly soaked did he retire to wash himself dry. But as soon as he heard the water gurgling out the drain he was back, waiting with impatience until he could jump in without fear of drowning. Paddling happily, he would get himself soaked all over again while I toweled myself dry.

In other ways he was peculiar.

Due to a neurological disorder, I tended to trip over things, and whenever I did Rrou always seemed to give me an anxious look. The first time I fell and he hurried to stand at my side I told myself it was just coincidence, even though I knew that normally a cat would bolt away from the thud of a falling body. But the second time he actually came running, with such a worried look in his eyes that I found myself giving him words of reassurance.

"It's all right, Rrou. I'm not hurt."

What kind of a changeling was he?

Incorrigibly curious, he had to inspect everything. The plumber trying to fix a leak in the faucet found it impossible to work because Rrou's nose kept getting in the way. Nor could he be lured away with his favorite snack. "Go away!" his distracted eyes told me. "Can't you see? I've got to find out what this man is doing."

Whatever package came into the house had to be examined, as well as whatever might be in my hands or on my dinner plate. With his paw extended much like a finger he would point to what had captured his attention, the gesture saying quite clearly, "What have you got there?"

To satisfy him I would put down a morsel from my plate, and the sensitive paw would just barely touch it, then gently push it this way and that, slowly draw it closer for more critical inspection, then like as not pass judgment by giving it a decent burial under anything movable nearby.

The paw was also adept at opening doors, flinging them imperiously either way if they were not securely latched. The house would become unaccountably cold, the heat turned up and up, until I remembered and looked, and found the outside door wide open. One most favored was the bathroom's because the hinges needed oiling. More than once a visitor was struck dumb in the middle of a sentence by a terrible shriek, to gaze at me in alarm until I explained, "It was only Rrou, opening a door."

Counteracting his one monstrous fault, Rrou had many virtues. He never begged. When hungry he merely sat beside his empty dish looking doleful. He never broke anything, or stole anything, or spilled anything. From the height of the wardrobe, where he liked to lie in wait so he could startle all who passed below by tapping the tops of their heads, he would leap to a table ten feet away and land on the one small uncluttered spot without disturbing even a pencil.

He was obedient, never once jumping on the forbidden table where food was prepared. He was almost overzealously clean. The tiniest of crumbs fallen off his plate had to be cleaned up before he would continue eating. He never failed to use his litter box. Because of his propensity for mayhem, he was not allowed outside, but this was no problem. He accepted the stricture without protest, never asked to be let out, never tried to get out.

He was, in fact, just about perfect, except for that terrible flaw that every so often turned him into a monster. I knew he was fond of me. Actually, the biting and scratching seemed to be his way of showing fondness. Was there any way of transforming it into behavior more acceptable?

I tried saying "no" and giving him a slap. In righteous anger he bit harder. I said "no" again and slapped again. After a few such battles he began to comprehend, but controlling the impulse was difficult. Whenever I saw a gleam in his eye that warned me he was about to attack I would quickly say "No," and he'd try to hold back, then give way to temptation in a rush, wincing even as he bit, anticipating the slap that would follow.

Learning that word "no" evidently convinced him that other sounds I made might also have meaning, and a number of useful words were added to his vocabulary. Of these "Say hello" was the most beneficial, for it persuaded him to respond graciously to being petted, thus bringing about improved relations with visitors, while "Excuse me" was most convenient to ask him to get out of the way, or remove himself from the chair I wished to sit on.

To all his other peculiarities there has now been added the ritual we must go through at bedtime. Standing at the foot of the bed, he looks over his shoulder to signal that he wishes to be covered. When I throw a blanket over him the mound thus created slowly subsides to a barely discernible rising and falling of his breathing, and there he stays until I turn out the light. Then, only then, just then, he crawls out of his bed to join me on mine, where he lies the whole night through without stirring, unless I turn around and he has to crawl over me to get to the other side.

So the cat who was such a problem has become so nearly perfect that it worries me. Ah, but he still has that one saving flaw. He still bites. Not hard, though, but quite gently, almost tenderly, never leaving a mark. I tell myself this is his own, his very own special way of saying, "I love you."

🐾🐾🐾🐾

A Gathering of Cats

About the Author

ERA ZISTEL, born in Cleveland, Ohio, worked briefly in the theater and on television before becoming a writer. She and her late husband moved from New York City to a tiny village in the Catskills, to live in a house surrounded by fourteen acres of virgin forest. Ms. Zistel has written dozens of books about her life with the animals who share her land. To protect that last remnant of wilderness from the onslaught of developers and the threat of hunters, she turned the land over to the town with the stipulation that it remain forever wild. Thus the ancient trees, the deer and the small animals—including a large flock of wild turkeys—will live unmolested in the small sanctuary called "The Zistel Woods," where the author acts as caretaker.

❧❧❧❧

About the Publisher

J. N. TOWNSEND PUBLISHING was started in 1986 by Jeremy Townsend in order to bring to the public's attention works of literature about living with animals. It is the publisher's wish that these books will promote humane and respectful treatment of animals and the world we share.

If you'd like more information about our books, or a free catalog, please write to:

J. N. Townsend Publishing
Dept. CAT
12 Greenleaf Drive
Exeter, NH 03833

🐾🐾🐾🐾